THE PLEASURES OF
IGNORANCE

THE PLEASURES OF IGNORANCE

BY

ROBERT LYND

KENNIKAT PRESS
Port Washington, N. Y./London

TO

JAMES WINDER GOOD

THE PLEASURES OF IGNORANCE

First published in 1921
Reissued in 1970 by Kennikat Press
Library of Congress Catalog Card No: 75-108702
SBN 8046-0923-3

Manufactured by Taylor Publishing Company   Dallas, Texas

ESSAY AND GENERAL LITERATURE INDEX REPRINT SERIES

CONTENTS

9

CONTENTS

*Acknowledgments are due to " The New Statesman,"
in which all but one of these essays appeared.
"Going to the Derby" appeared in " The Daily
News."—R. L.*

I

THE
PLEASURES OF IGNORANCE

It is impossible to take a walk in the country with an average townsman—especially, perhaps, in April or May—without being amazed at the vast continent of his ignorance. It is impossible to take a walk in the country oneself without being amazed at the vast continent of one's own ignorance. Thousands of men and women live and die without knowing the difference between a beech and an elm, between the song of a thrush and the song of a blackbird. Probably in a modern city the man who can distinguish between a thrush's and a blackbird's song is the exception. It is not that we have not seen the birds. It is simply that we have not noticed them. We have been surrounded by birds all our lives, yet so feeble is our observation that many of us could not tell whether or not the chaffinch sings, or the colour of the cuckoo. We argue

11

like small boys as to whether the cuckoo always sings as he flies or sometimes in the branches of a tree—whether Chapman drew on his fancy or his knowledge of nature in the lines:

When in the oak's green arms the cuckoo
     sings,
And first delights men in the lovely springs.

This ignorance, however, is not altogether miserable. Out of it we get the constant pleasure of discovery. Every fact of nature comes to us each spring, if only we are sufficiently ignorant, with the dew still on it. If we have lived half a lifetime without having ever even seen a cuckoo, and know it only as a wandering voice, we are all the more delighted at the spectacle of its runaway flight as it hurries from wood to wood conscious of its crimes, and at the way in which it halts hawk-like in the wind, its long tail quivering, before it dares descend on a hill-side of fir-trees where avenging presences may lurk. It would be absurd to pretend that the naturalist does not also find pleasure in observing the life of the birds, but his is a steady pleasure, almost a sober and plodding occupation, compared to the morning enthusiasm of the man who sees a cuckoo for the first time, and, behold, the world is made new.

And, as to that, the happiness even of the naturalist depends in some measure upon his ignorance, which still leaves him new worlds of this kind to conquer. He may have reached the very Z of knowledge in the books, but he still feels half ignorant until he has confirmed each bright particular with his eyes. He wishes with his own eyes to see the female cuckoo—rare spectacle!—as she lays her egg on the ground and takes it in her bill to the nest in which it is destined to breed infanticide. He would sit day after day with a field-glass against his eyes in order personally to endorse or refute the evidence suggesting that the cuckoo *does* lay on the ground and not in a nest. And, if he is so far fortunate as to discover this most secretive of birds in the very act of laying, there still remain for him other fields to conquer in a multitude of such disputed questions as whether the cuckoo's egg is always of the same colour as the other eggs in the nest in which she abandons it. Assuredly the men of science have no reason as yet to weep over their lost ignorance. If they seem to know everything, it is only because you and I know almost nothing. There will always be a fortune of ignorance waiting for them under every fact they turn up. They will never know what song the Sirens sang to Ulysses any more than Sir Thomas Browne did.

If I have called in the cuckoo to illustrate the ordinary man's ignorance, it is not because I can speak with authority on that bird. It is simply because, passing the spring in a parish that seemed to have been invaded by all the cuckoos of Africa, I realised how exceedingly little I, or anybody else I met, knew about them. But your and my ignorance is not confined to cuckoos. It dabbles in all created things, from the sun and moon down to the names of the flowers. I once heard a clever lady asking whether the new moon always appears on the same day of the week. She added that perhaps it is better not to know, because, if one does not know when or in what part of the sky to expect it, its appearance is always a pleasant surprise. I fancy, however, the new moon always comes as a surprise even to those who are familiar with her time-tables.

And it is the same with the coming in of spring and the waves of the flowers. We are not the less delighted to find an early primrose because we are sufficiently learned in the services of the year to look for it in March or April rather than in October. We know, again, that the blossom precedes and not succeeds the fruit of the apple-tree, but this does not lessen our amazement at the beautiful holiday of a May orchard.

At the same time there is, perhaps, a special pleasure in re-learning the names of many of the flowers every spring. It is like re-reading a book that one has almost forgotten. Montaigne tells us that he had so bad a memory that he could always read an old book as though he had never read it before. I have myself a capricious and leaking memory. I can read *Hamlet* itself and *The Pickwick Papers* as though they were the work of new authors and had come wet from the press, so much of them fades between one reading and another. There are occasions on which a memory of this kind is an affliction, especially if one has a passion for accuracy. But this is only when life has an object beyond entertainment. In respect of mere luxury, it may be doubted whether there is not as much to be said for a bad memory as for a good one. With a bad memory one can go on reading Plutarch and *The Arabian Nights* all one's life. Little shreds and tags, it is probable, will stick even in the worst memory, just as a succession of sheep cannot leap through a gap in a hedge without leaving a few wisps of wool on the thorns. But the sheep themselves escape, and the great authors leap in the same way out of an idle memory and leave little enough behind.

And, if we can forget books, it is as easy to forget the months and what they showed us, when once they are gone. Just for the moment I tell myself that I know May like the multiplication table and could pass an examination on its flowers, their appearance and their order. To-day I can affirm confidently that the buttercup has five petals. (Or is it six? I knew for certain last week.) But next year I shall probably have forgotten my arithmetic, and may have to learn once more not to confuse the buttercup with the celandine. Once more I shall see the world as a garden through the eyes of a stranger, my breath taken away with surprise by the painted fields. I shall find myself wondering whether it is science or ignorance which affirms that the swift (that black exaggeration of the swallow and yet a kinsman of the humming-bird) never settles even on a nest, but disappears at night into the heights of the air. I shall learn with fresh astonishment that it is the male, and not the female, cuckoo that sings. I may have to learn again not to call the campion a wild geranium, and to rediscover whether the ash comes early or late in the etiquette of the trees. A contemporary English novelist was once asked by a foreigner what was the most important crop in England. He answered without a moment's hesitation : " Rye." Ignorance so complete as this seems to me to be touched with magnificence ; but the ignorance even of illiterate persons is enormous. The average man who uses a telephone could not explain how a telephone works. He takes for granted the telephone, the railway train, the linotype, the aeroplane, as our grandfathers took for granted the miracles of the gospels. He neither questions nor understands them. It is as though each of us investigated and made his own only a tiny circle of facts. Knowledge outside the day's work is regarded by most men as a gewgaw. Still we are constantly in reaction against our ignorance. We rouse ourselves at intervals and speculate. We revel in speculations about anything at all—about life after death or about such questions as that which is said to have puzzled Aristotle, "why sneezing from noon to midnight was good, but from night to noon unlucky." One of the greatest joys known to man is to take such a flight into ignorance in search of knowledge. The great pleasure of ignorance is, after all, the pleasure of asking questions. The man who has lost this pleasure or exchanged it for the pleasure of dogma, which is the pleasure of answering, is already beginning to stiffen. One envies so inquisitive a man as Jowett, who sat down to the study of physiology in his sixties. Most of us have lost the sense of our ignorance long before that age. We even become vain of our squirrel's hoard of knowledge and regard increasing age itself as a school of omniscience. We forget that Socrates was famed for wisdom not because he was omniscient but because he realised at the age of seventy that he still knew nothing.

II

THE HERRING FLEET

THE last spectacle of which Christian men are likely to grow tired is a harbour. Centuries hence there may be jumping-off places for the stars, and our children's children's and so forth children may regard a ship as a creeping thing scarcely more adventurous than a worm. Meanwhile, every harbour gives us a sense of being in touch, if not with the ends of the universe, with the ends of the earth. This, more than the entrance to a wood or the source of a river or the top of a bald hill, is the beginning of infinity. Even the dirtiest coal-boat that lies beached in the harbour, a mere hulk of utilities that are taken away by dirty men in dirty carts, will in a day or two lift itself from the mud on a full tide and float away like a spirit into the sunset or curtsy to the image of the North Star. Mystery lies over the sea. Every ship is bound for Thule. That, perhaps, is why men are content day after day to stand on the pier-head and to gaze at the water and the ships and sailors running up and down the decks and pulling the ropes of sails.

We may have no reason for pretending to ourselves that the fishing-boats are ships of dreams setting out on infinite voyages. But, none the less, even in a fishing village there is always a congregation of watching men and women on the pier. Every day the crowd collects to see the harbour awake into life with the bustle of men about to set out among the nations of the fishes. By day the boats lie side by side in the harbour—stand side by side, rather, like horses in a stable. There are two rows of them, making a camp of masts on the shallow water. In other parts of the harbour white gigs are bottomed on the sand in companies of two and three. As the tide slowly rises, the masts which have been lying over on one side in a sleepy stillness begin to stir, then to sway, until with each new impulse of the sea all the boats are dancing, and soon the whole harbour is awake and merry as if every mast were a steeple with a peal of bells. It is not long till the fishermen arrive. One

er-   every cobbled lane. How
ws   ne noise made by a man in
of   the stones! Surely, he strikes
              he road. He thumps the ground
re   mmer. The earth rings. One has
n   boots in the morning hanging out-
              or of his house while he slept. They
s   oiled, and left there to dry. They
             t the shape of his limb and the crook
             nee in an uncanny way. They look as
             he had taken off his legs before going
             he house and hung them on the wall.
             he fisherman is a hero not only in his
             .   His sea-coat is no less magnificent.
           may be of oil-skin yellow or of maroon
          of stained white or of blue, with a blue
         sey showing under it, and, perhaps, a red
         ollen muffler or a scarf with green spots on
a red ground round his throat. He has not
learned to be timid of colour. Even out of
the mouths of his boots you may see the ends
of red knitted leggings protruding. His yellow
or black sou'-wester roofing the back of his
neck, he comes down to harbour, as splendid
as a figure at a fair. And always, when he
arrives, he is smoking a pipe. As one watches

him, one wonders if anybody except a fish
man, as he looks out over the harbour, know
how to smoke. He has made tobacco part
himself, like breathing.

If the tide is already full the fishermen a
taken off in small rowing-boats, most of the
standing, and the place is busy with a criss
cross of travelling crews till the fishing-boat
are all manned. If the water is not yet deep
however, most of the men walk to their boats,
lumbering through the waves, and occasionally
jumping like a wading girl as a larger wave
threatens the tops of their boots. Many of
them carry their supper in a basket or a hand-
kerchief. The first of the boats begins to move
out of its stall. It is tugged into the clear
water, and the fishermen put out long oars
and row it laboriously to the mouth of the
harbour and the wind. It is followed by a
motor-boat, and another, and another. There
are forty putting up their sails like one. The
harbour moves. One has a sense as of things
liberated. It is as though a flock of birds
were being loosed into the air — as though
pigeon after pigeon were being set free
out of a basket for home. Lug-sail after lug-

sail, brown as the underside of a mushroom, hurries out among the waves. A green little tub of a steamboat follows with insolent smoke. The motor-boats hasten out like scenting dogs. Every sort of craft—motor-boat, gig, lugger and steamboat—makes for sea, higgledy-piggledy in a long line, an irregular procession of black and blue and green and white and brown. Here, as in the men's clothes, the paint-pots have been spilled.

There is nothing more sociable than a fishing-fleet. The boats overtake each other, like horses in a race. They gallop in rivalry. But for the most part they keep together, and move like a travelling town over the sea. As likely as not they will have to come back out of the storm into the shelter of the bay, and they will ride there till nightfall, when every boat becomes a lamp and every sail a shadow. In the darkness they hang like a constellation on the oily water. They become a company of dancing stars. Every now and then a boat moves off on a quest of its own. It is as though the firmament were shaken. One hears the kick-kick-kick of the motor, and a star has become a will-o'-the-wisp. These lights can no more keep still than a playground of children. They always make a pattern on the water, but they never make the same pattern. Sometimes they lengthen themselves against the sandy shore on the far side of the bay into a golden river. Sometimes they huddle together into a little procession of monks carrying tapers. . . .

One goes down to the harbour after breakfast the next morning to see what has been the result of the night's fishing. One does not really need to go down. One can see it afar off. There is movement as at the building of a city. On every boat men are busy emptying the nets, disentangling the fish that have been caught by the gills, tumbling them in a liquid mass into the bottom of the boat. One can hardly see the fish separately. They flow into one another. They are a pool of quicksilver. One is amazed, as the disciples must have been amazed at the miraculous draught. Everything is covered with their scales. The fishermen are spotted as if with confetti. Their hands, their brown coats, their boots are a mass of white-and-blue spots. The labourers with the gurries—great blue boxes that are carried like Sedan-chairs between two pairs of handles

—come up alongside, and the fish are ladled into the gurries from tin pans. As each gurry is filled the men hasten off with it to where the auctioneer is standing. With the help of a small notebook and a lead pencil he auctions it before an outsider can wink, and the gurry is taken a few yards further, where women are pouring herrings into barrels. They, too, are covered with fish-scales from head to foot. They are dabbled like a painter's palette. So great is the haul that every cart in the country-side has come down to lend a hand. The fish are poured into the carts over the sides of the boats like water. Old fishermen stand aside and look on with a sense of having wasted their youth. They recall the time when they went fishing in the North Sea and had to be content to sell their catch at a shilling and sixpence a cran—a cran being equal to four gurries, or about a thousand herrings. Who is there now who would sell even a hundred herrings for one and sixpence? Who is there who would sell a hundred herrings for ten and sixpence? Yet one gig alone this morning has brought in fourteen thousand herrings. No wonder that there is an atmosphere of excitement in the harbour. No wonder that the carts almost run over you as they make journey after journey between boat and barrel. No wonder that three different sorts of sea-gulls — the herring gull, the lesser black-headed gull, and the black-backed gull—have gathered about us in screaming multitudes and fill the air like a snowstorm. Every child in the town seems to be making for home with its finger in a fish's mouth, or in two fishes' mouths, or in three fishes' mouths. Artists have hurried down to the harbour, and have set up their easels on every spot that is not al-ready occupied by a fish barrel or an auctioneer or a man with a knife in his teeth preparing to gut a dogfish. The town has lost its head. It has become Midas for the day. Every time it opens its mouth a herring comes out. A doom of herrings has come upon us. The smell rises to heaven. It is as though we were breathing fish-scales. Even the pretty blue overalls of the children have become spotted. Every-where barrels and boxes have been piled high. We are hoisting them on to carts—farm carts, grocers' carts, coal carts, any sort of carts. We must get rid of the stuff at all costs.

THE HERRING FLEET

Anything to get it up the hill to the railway station. The very horses are frenzied. They stick their toes into the hill and groan. The drivers, excited with cupidity as they think of all the journeys they will be able to make before evening, bully them and beat them with the end of the reins. Their eyes are excited, their gestures impatient. They fill the town with clamour and smell. It is an occasion on which, as the vulgar say, they wouldn't call the Queen their aunt. . . .

This, I fancy, is where all the romance of the sea began—in the story of a greedy man and a fresh herring. The ship was a symbol of man's questing stomach long before it was a symbol of his questing soul. He was a hungry man, not a poet, when he built the first harbour. Luckily, the harbour made a poet of him. Sails gave him wings. He learned to traffic for wonders. He became a traveller. He told tales. He discovered the illusion of horizons. Perhaps, however, it is less the sailor than the ship that attracts our imagination. The ship seems to convey to us more than anything else a sense at once of perfect freedom and perfect adventure.

PLEASURES OF IGNORANCE

That is why we are content to stand on the harbour stones all day and watch anything with sails. We ourselves want to live in some such freedom and adventure as this. We are feeding our appetite for liberty as we gaze hungrily after the ships making their way out of harbour into the sea.

III

THE BETTING MAN

IF The Panther wins the Derby,[1] as most
people apparently expect him to do, his victory
will carry more weight among frequenters of
race-courses as an argument for Socialism than
any that has yet been invented. For The
Panther is a Government-bred horse, born and
brought up in defiance of the *laissez-faire*
principles of Mr Harold Cox. He will therefore carry the colours of a great principle at
Epsom as well as those of his present lessee.
Who would have thought five years ago that
the Derby favourite of 1919 would start under
so grave a responsibility?

Not that racing men have much time to
spare for thoughts about social problems, even
when these are related to a horse. Theirs is a
busy life. They enjoy little of the leisure that
falls to the lot of statesmen and haberdashers.

[1] He didn't.

Their anxieties are a serial story continued from one edition of the day's papers to another. Nor does the last edition of the evening paper make an end of their anxieties. It is not an epilogue to one day so much as a prologue to the next. The programme of races for the following day suggests more problems than the Peace Conference itself could settle in a month. The racing man, having studied the names of the horses entered, goes out to buy some tobacco. As he takes his change from the tobacconist, he asks: " Have you heard anything for to-morrow?" The tobacconist says: " I heard Green Cloak for the first race." The racing man nods. " You didn't hear anything for the big race?" he asks. " No. Somebody was saying Holy Saint." " I heard Oily Hair," says the racing man gravely. " Good-night." And he goes out. His brow becomes knitted with thought as he moves off along the pavement. He tells himself that Holy Saint certainly does offer difficulties. Holy Saint is a notoriously bad starter. If he could be trusted to get away, he would be one of the finest horses of his year in long-distance races. But he is continually being left at the post. To back him would be pure gambling. He could win if he liked, but would he like? On the whole, Oily Hair is a safer horse to back. He has already beaten Holy Saint in the Chiswick Cup, and only lost the Scotch Plate to Disaster by a neck. As the racing man allows his memory to dwell on the achievements of Oily Hair his confidence rises. " I see nothing to beat him," he says to himself. He has just decided to put "a fiver" on him when he meets an acquaintance, who suggests a drink. As they drink, the talk turns on horses. "What are you backing in the big race to-morrow?" "Have you heard anything?" " I heard Oily Hair." " I think not. I'll tell you why. Tommy Fitzgibbon's youngest sister is at school with two sisters of Willie Soames, who's going to ride Peace on Earth to-morrow, and one of them told her that Willie had written to her to put every halfpenny she has on Peace on Earth." " I'm sick, sore and tired of backing Peace on Earth. He's a cantankerous beast that seems to take a positive pleasure in losing races." "Well, remember what I told you. . . ."

On arriving home our sportsman goes to his

shelves and takes down the last annual volume of *M'Call's Racing Chronicle and Pocket Turf Calendar,* and looks up Peace on Earth in the index. He turns up the record of one race after another, and finds that the horse has a better past than he had remembered. He cannot make up his mind what to do. He looks over several weekly papers to see if any of them can throw light on his difficulties. Each of them names a different winner for the big race. When he puts on his pyjamas that night, all he knows is that he has decided to decide nothing till the next day.

Next day he once more reads the names of the horses entered for the various races, and glances down the list of winners selected by the racing prophet in the morning paper. Having breakfasted late, he finds he has only about an hour to waste before catching a train for the races, and he resolves to pay a call at the "Bird of Paradise," where a friend of his who has an unusual gift for picking up information is usually to be found about noon. He learns from the landlord that his friend has been in and gone away, but the landlord tells him that he hears Pudding is a certainty.

THE BETTING MAN

"Have you any reason for thinking so?"
"Well, there was a man in here who has a son
a policeman close by Jobson's stables, and he
tells me that everybody in the neighbourhood
has been backing Pudding down to their last
spoon. That looks as if word had been passed
round that it was going to win." The racing
man passes out and looks in at the "Pink
Elephant" to see if his friend is there. He
is seated at a little table in an upstairs parlour
with four others, all drinking whisky and
exchanging tips. They belong to the most
credulous race of men alive. They are all
believers in what is called information, and
information is simply the betting man's name
for gossip. The friend is speaking in a low but
excited voice to his companions, who crouch
over towards him in order to catch information
not meant for the rest of the room. He tells
how he had just been in to buy a paper at his
newsagent's, and how his newsagent had been
calling on his solicitor that morning, and the
solicitor told him that the caller who had just
left as he came in was Gordon, the owner of
Cutandrun, and Gordon said that Cutandrun
was the biggest thing that had ever come into

his hands. The buzz-buzz of talk in the smoke-filled room and the clatter of passing carts makes it difficult to hear him, but the others lean over the table with red, intent faces, like men among whom an apostle has come. They do not stay long over their drinks, as they have not much time for social pleasures. They swallow their whisky with a quick gesture, look at their watches, stand up hurriedly and part with handshakes.

Then comes a drive to the railway station, where race-cards are being sold. The racing-man buys a "card" and several papers. He looks down the lists of the horses again in the train, and tries to make up his mind whether to take the tobacconist's tip and back Green Cloak for the first race. He believes greatly in breeding, and by far the best-bred horse in the race is Liberal, who has three Derby winners in his pedigree. Then there is Red Rose, who created a sensation a month ago by winning two races in a day. He decides to do nothing till he sees the horses themselves. He pays thirty shillings at the turnstile of the race-course and is admitted to the grand stand. Already one or two bookmakers are shouting from their stands, and some of them have chalked up on blackboards the odds they are willing to give in the big race. He looks at the board and sees that he can get twenties against Cutandrun. A five-pound note might bring him a hundred pounds. On the other hand, if Oily Hair was going to win, he wouldn't like to miss it. The bookmakers are offering fives against it. Holy Saint is hot favourite at two to one. That alone makes him impatient of it, for he dislikes backing favourites. He prefers the big risks, with great scoops if he wins. However, he will make up his mind later. Meanwhile, he will go to the paddock and have a look at the horses for the first race. Half-a-dozen horses are already out, and men with numbers on their arms are walking them round and round in a ring. He consults his card and sees that No. 7 is Brighton Beauty, and No. 2 (a slender, glossy, black beast with a white star in his forehead) Green Cloak. Liberal has not appeared. The numbers of the starters, with the names of the jockeys, are now being hoisted. He makes a pencil-mark opposite the name of each starter on his racing-card, and jots down the name of the jockey. Raff, he sees, is riding Green Cloak. That is in its favour.

When he gets back to the betting-ring, the bookmakers are shouting hoarsely against each other. Liberal is a very hot favourite. They are shouting: "I'll take two to one. I'll take two to one. Five to one bar one. A hundred to eight Green Cloak." He feels almost sure Liberal will win, but Green Cloak—he wishes he had asked the tobacconist where he got his information from. Anyhow, half-a-sovereign doesn't matter much. He goes up to a bookmaker, and says: "Ten shillings Green Cloak." The bookmaker turns to his clerk and says: "Six pound five to ten shillings Green Cloak," gives a red-white-and-blue card with his name and a number on it; the other takes the card, writes on the back of it the name of the horse and the amount of the bet, and makes for the stand to see the race. The horses have now come out, and are off one after another to the starting-post. Green Cloak would be hard to miss because of his jockey's colours—old gold, scarlet sleeves, and green and black quartered cap. The bell has hardly rung to

THE BETTING MAN

announce that the race has begun when men in the crowd begin to dogmatise about the result. One man keeps saying: "Green Cloak wins this race. Green Cloak wins this race." Another says: "Liberal leads." Another says: "No; that's Jumping Frog." To the unaccustomed eye the horses seem as close to each other as a swarm of bees. Suddenly, however, a bay horse springs forward and seems to put a length between itself and the others at every stride. The people in the stand shout: "Liberal! Liberal!" It wins by about ten lengths. Green Cloak is second, but a bad second. The crowd begins to pour down from the stand again. Those who have won wait near the bookmakers till the winner has been to the unsaddling enclosure and the announcement "All right" is made. Then the bookmakers begin to pay out, and the crowd moves off to the paddock again to see the horses for the next race.

Friends stop each other and exchange information in low voices. Others do their best to listen in the hope of overhearing information: "I hear Tomsk," "Johnnie says lay your last penny on Glasgow Pet," "I'm going

37

to back Submarine." And the parade of the horses, the hoisting of the names of the starters and jockeys, the laying of the bets, and the climbing of the grand stand are all gone through over and over again. The betting man has no time even for a drink. To the casual onlooker a day's horse-racing has the appearance of a day's holiday. But the racing man knows better. He is collecting information, coming to decisions, wandering among the bookies in the hope of getting a good price, climbing into the grand stand and descending from it, studying the points of the horses all the time with as little chance of leisure as though he were a stockbroker during a financial crisis or a sailor on a sinking ship.

Perhaps, in the train on the way home from the races, he may relax a little. Certainly, if he has backed Cutandrun, he will. For Cutandrun won at ten to one, and his pocket is full of five-pound notes. He feels quite jocular now that the strain is over. He makes puns on the names of the defeated horses. "Lie Low lay low all right," he announces to the compartment, indifferent to the scowls of the man in the corner who had backed it. "Hop-

scotch didn't hop quite fast enough." Were
he tipsy, he could not jest more fluently. His
jokes are small, but be not too severe on him.
The man has had a hard day. Wait but an
hour, and care will descend on him again.
He will not have sat down to dinner in his
hotel for three minutes till someone will be
saying to him : " Have you heard anything for
the Cup to-morrow ? " There is no six-hours
day for the betting man. He is the drudge
of chance for every waking hour. He is
enviable only for one thing. He knows what
to talk about to barbers.

IV

THE HUM OF INSECTS

It makes all the difference whether you hear an insect in the bedroom or in the garden. In the garden the voice of the insect soothes; in the bedroom it irritates. In the garden it is the hum of spring; in the bedroom it seems to belong to the same school of music as the bizz of the dentist's drill or the saw-mill. It may be that it is not the right sort of insect that invades the bedroom. Even in the garden we wave away a mosquito. Either its note is in itself offensive or we dislike it as the voice of an unscrupulous enemy. By an unscrupulous enemy I mean an enemy that attacks without waiting to be attacked. The mosquito is a beast of prey; it is out for blood, whether one is as gentle as Tom Pinch or uses violence. The bee and the wasp are in comparison noble creatures. They will, so it is said, never injure a human being unless a

human being has injured them. The worst of
it is, they do not discriminate between one
human being and another, and the bee that
floats over the wall into our garden may turn
out to have been exasperated by the behaviour
of a retired policeman five miles away who
struck at it with a spade and roused in it a
blind passion for reprisals. That or something
like it is, probably, the explanation of the
stings perfectly innocent persons receive from
an insect that is said never to touch you if you
leave it alone. As a matter of fact, when a
bee loses its head, it does not even wait for a
human being in order to relieve its feelings.
I have seen a dog racing round a field in terror
as a result of a sting from an angry bee. I
have seen a turkey racing round a farmyard in
terror as a result of the same thing. All the
trouble arose from a human being's having
very properly removed a large quantity of
honey from a row of hives. I do not
admit that the bee would have been justified
in stinging even the human being—who,
after all, is master on this partially civilised
planet. It had certainly no right to sting the
dog or the turkey, which had as little to do

with stealing the honey as the Vice-Chancellor of Oxford University. Yet in spite of such things, and of the fact that some breeds of bees are notorious for their crossness, especially when there is thunder in the air, the bee is morally far higher in the scale than the mosquito. Not only does it give you honey instead of malaria, and help your apples and strawberries to multiply, but it aims at living a quiet, inoffensive life, at peace with everybody, except when it is annoyed. The mosquito does what it does in cold blood. That is why it is so unwelcome a bedroom visitor.

But even a bee or a wasp, I fancy, would seem tedious company at two in the morning, especially if it came and buzzed near the pillow. It is not so much that you would be frightened : if the wasp alighted on your cheek, you could always lie still and hold your breath till it had finished trying to sting—that is an infallible preventive. But there is a limit to the amount of your night's rest that you are willing to sacrifice in this way. You cannot hold your breath while you are asleep, and yet you dare not cease holding your breath while a wasp is walking over your face. Besides, it

42

might crawl into your ear, and what would you do then? Luckily, the question does not often arise in practice owing to the fact that the wasp and the bee are more like human beings than mosquitoes and have more or less the same habits of nocturnal rest. As we sit in the garden, however, the mind is bound to speculate, and to revolve such questions as whether this hum of insects that delights us is in itself delightful, whether its delightfulness depends on its surroundings, or whether it depends on its associations with past springs.

Certainly in a garden the noise of insects seems as essentially beautiful a thing as the noise of birds or the noise of the sea. Even these have been criticised, especially by persons who suffer from sleeplessness, but their beauty is affirmed by the general voice of mankind. These three noises appear to have an infinite capacity for giving us pleasure—a capacity, probably, beyond that of any music of instruments. It may be that on hearing them we become a part of some universal music, and that the rhythm of wave, bird and insect echoes in some way the rhythm of our own breath and blood. Man is in love with life, and these are the millionfold chorus of life— the magnified echo of his own pleasure in being alive. At the same time, our pleasure in the hum of insects is also, I think, a pleasure of reminiscence. It reminds us of other springs and summers in other gardens. It reminds us of the infinite peace of childhood when on a fine day the world hardly existed beyond the garden-gate. We can smell moss-roses—how we loved them as children!—as a bee swings by. Insect after insect dances through the air, each dying away like a note of music, and we see again the border of pinks and the strawberries, and the garden paths edged with box, and the old dilapidated wooden seat under the tree, and an apple-tree in the long grass, and a stream beyond the apple-tree, and all those things that made us infinitely happy as children when we were in the country—happier than we were ever made by toys, for we do not remember any toys so intensely as we remember the garden and the farm. We had the illusion in those days that it was going to last for ever. There was no past or future. There was nothing real

44

except the present in which we lived—a present
in which all the human beings were kind, in
which a dim-sighted grandfather sang songs
(especially a song in which the chorus began
" Free and easy"), in which aunts brought us
animal biscuits out of town, in which there
was neither man-servant nor maid-servant,
neither ox nor ass, that did not seem to go
about with a bright face.   It was a present that
overflowed with kindness, though everybody
except the ox and the ass believed that it was
only by the skin of our teeth that any of us
would escape being burnt alive for eternity.
Perhaps we thought little enough about it except on Sundays or at prayers.   Certainly no one
was gloomy about it before children.   William
John McNabb, the huge labourer who looked
after the horses, greeted us all as cheerfully as
if we had been saved and ready for paradise.

It would be unfair to human beings, however, to suggest that they are less lavish with
their smiles than they were thirty years or so
ago.   Everybody—or almost everybody—still
smiles.   We can hardly stop to talk to a man
in the street without a duet of smiles.   The
Prince of Wales smiles across the world from

left to right, and the Crown Prince of Japan smiles across the world from right to left. We cannot open an illustrated paper without seeing smiling statesmen, cricketers, jockeys, oarsmen, bridegrooms, clergymen, actresses and undergraduates. Yet somehow we are no longer made happy by a smile. We no longer take it, as we used to take it, as evidence that the person smiling is either happy or kind. It then seemed to come from the heart. It now seems a formula. It is, we may admit, a pleasant and useful formula. But a man might easily be a burglar or a murderer or a Cabinet Minister and smile. Some people are supposed to smile merely in order to show what good teeth they have. William John McNabb, I am sure, never did that.

We need not grumble at our contemporaries, however, for not being so fine as William John McNabb. To children, for all we know, the world may still seem to be full of people who laugh because they are happy and smile because they are kind. The world will always remain to a child the chief of toys, and the hum of insects as enchanting as the hum of a musical top. Even those of us who are grown up can recover this enchantment, not only through the pleasures of memory but through the endless pleasures of watching the things that inhabit the earth. The world is always waiting to be discovered in full, and yet no life is long enough to discover the whole of a single county, or even the whole of a single parish. Who alive, for instance, knows all the moles of Sussex? I confess I got my first sight of one a few days ago, and, though I had seen dead moles hanging from trees and had read descriptions of moles, the living creature was as unexpected as if one had come on it silent upon a peak in Darien. I had never expected it to look so black and glossy in the midday sun or to have that little pink snout that made me think of it as a small underground pig. I had always been told, too, that the sound of a footstep would frighten a mole, but this mole only began to show fright at the sound of voices. Then it began to tear its way into the undergrowth with paws and snout ever trying to overtake each other. Mr Blunden has described how

The lost mole tries to pierce the mattocked clay
In agony and terror of the sun.

PLEASURES OF IGNORANCE

I got much the same impression of agony and
terror as this poor creature dug its way into
the grass and ferns and, coming out at the far
end of the clump, bolted under a tree like a
frightened pig. And yet, they say, this poor
little coward is a fierce animal enough. He
is, we are told, impelled by so cruel a hunger
that he would die of it were it to go unsatisfied
for even twenty-four hours. If he can find
nothing else to eat, he will kill and eat a
fellow-mole. So the authorities tell us, but
I wonder how many of the authorities have
even seen a mole in the very act of canni-
balism. How many of them have followed
him on his long journeys through the bowels
of the earth? He certainly looked no South
Sea monster on the Sunday morning on which
for a few seconds I watched him. Nor would
John Clare have written affectionately about
him had he been entirely bloody-minded.

Then there was the hedgehog. The charm
of hedgehogs is that we do not see them
every day—that their appearance is a secret
and an accident. They are a part of the busy
life that goes on all about us as mysteriously
as the movements of spirits. Consequently,

48

when I was looking over a sloping field the other evening and, hearing a crackling as of sticks being trodden on, turned my eyes and saw a living creature making its way out of a wood into the grass, I was delighted to find that it was a hedgehog and not a man or a rat. I could see it only dimly in the twilight, and it was difficult to believe that so small an animal had made so great a noise. The pleasure of recognition, unfortunately, was not mutual. No sooner did the hedgehog hear a foot pressing on the road than it gave up all thoughts of its supper of insects and hobbled back into the thicket. I regretted only that I had not made a greater noise and scared it into rolling itself into a ball, as everybody says it does when alarmed. But it is perhaps just as well that the hedgehog did not merely repeat itself in this way. We like a certain variety of behaviour in animals—some element of the unexpected that always keeps our curiosity alive and looking forward.

But we must not exaggerate the pleasure to be got from moles and hedgehogs. They make a part of our being happy, but they do not delight the whole of our being, as a child is delighted by the world every spring. It is probably the child in us that responds most wholeheartedly to such pleasures. They, like the hum of insects, help to restore the illusion of a world that is perfectly happy because it is such a Noah's Ark of a spectacle and everybody is kind. But, even as we submit to the illusion in the garden, we become restive in our deck-chairs and remember the telephone or the daily paper or a letter that has to be written. And reality weighs on us, like a hand laid on a top, making an end of the spinning, making an end of the music. The world is no longer a toy dancing round and round. It is a problem, a run-down machine, a stuffy room, full of little stabbing creatures that make an irritating noise

V

CATS

THE Champion Cat Show has been held at the Crystal Palace, but the champion cat was not there. One could not possibly allow him to appear in public. He is for show, but not in a cage. He does not compete, because he is above competition. You know this as well as I. Probably you possess him. I certainly do. That is the supreme test of a cat's excellence —the test of possession. One does not say: "You should see Brailsford's cat" or "You should see Adcock's cat" or "You should see Sharp's cat," but "You should see our cat." There is nothing we are more egoistic about—not even children—than about cats. I have heard a man, for lack of anything better to boast about, boasting that his cat eats cheese. In anyone else's cat it would have seemed an inferior habit and only worth mentioning to the servant as a warning. But because the

51

cat happens to be his cat, this man talks about its vice excitedly among women as though it were an accomplishment. It is seldom that we hear a cat publicly reproached with guilt by anyone above a cook. He is not permitted to steal from our own larder. But if he visits the next-door house by stealth and returns over the wall with a Dover sole in his jaws, we really cannot help laughing. We are a little nervous at first, and our mirth is tinged with pity at the thought of the probably elderly and dyspeptic gentleman who has had his luncheon filched away almost from under his nose. If we were quite sure that it was from No. 14, and not from No. 9 or No. 11, that the fish had been stolen, we might — conceivably — call round and offer to pay for it. But with a cat one is never quite sure. And we cannot call round on all the neighbours and make a general announcement that our cat is a thief. In any case the next move lies with the wronged neighbour. As day follows day, and there is no sign of his irate and murder-bent figure advancing up the path, we recover our mental balance and begin to see the cat's exploit in a new light. We do not yet extol it on moral grounds, but undoubtedly, the more we think of it, the deeper becomes our admiration. Of the two great heroes of the Greeks we admire one for his valour and one for his cunning. The epic of the cat is the epic of Odysseus. The old gentleman with the Dover sole gradually assumes the aspect of a Polyphemus outwitted — outwitted and humiliated to the point of not even being able to throw things after his tormentor. Clever cat! Nobody else's cat could have done such a thing. We should like to celebrate the Rape of the Dover Sole in Latin verse.

As for the Achillean sort of prowess, we do not demand it of a cat, but we are proud of it when it exists. There is a pleasure in seeing strange cats fly at his approach, either in single file over the wall or in the scattered aimlessness of a bursting bomb. Theoretically, we hate him to fight, but, if he does fight and comes home with a torn ear, we have to summon up all the resources of our finer nature in order not to rejoice on noticing that the cat next door looks as though it had been through a railway accident. I am sorry for the cat next door. I hate him so, and it must be horrible to be hated. But he should not sit on my wall and look at me with yellow eyes. If his eyes were any other colour—even the blue that is now said to be the mark of the runaway husband—I feel certain I could just manage to endure him. But they are the sort of yellow eyes that you expect to see looking out at you from a hole in the panelling in a novel by Mr Sax Rohmer. The only reason why I am not frightened of them is that the cat is so obviously frightened of me. I never did him any injury unless to hate is to injure. But he lowers his head when I appear as though he expected to be guillotined. He does not run away : he merely crouches like a guilty thing. Perhaps he remembers how often he has stepped delicately over my seed-beds, but not so delicately as to leave no mark of ruin among the infant lettuces and the less-than-infant autumn-sprouting broccoli. These things I could forgive him, but it is not easy to forgive him the look in his eyes when he watches a bird at its song. They are ablaze with evil. He becomes a sort of Jack the Ripper at the opera. People tell us that we should not blame cats for this sort of thing—

that it is their nature and so forth. They even suggest, that a cat is no more cruel in eating robin than we are cruel ourselves in eating chicken. This seems to me to be quibbling. In the first place, there is an immense difference between a robin and a chicken. In the second place, we are willing to share our chicken with the cat—at least, we are willing to share the skin and such of the bones as are not required for soup. Besides, a cat has not the same need of delicacies as a human being. It can eat, and even digest, anything. It can eat the black skin of filleted plaice. It can eat the bits of gristle that people leave on the side of their plates. It can eat boiled cod. It can eat New Zealand mutton. There is no reason why an animal with so undiscriminating a palate should demand song-birds for its food, when even human beings, who are fairly unscrupulous eaters, have agreed in some measure to abstain from them. On reflection, however, I doubt if it is his appetite for birds that makes the cat with the yellow eyes feel guilty. If you were able to talk to him in his own language, and formulate your accusations against him as a bird-eater, he would probably be merely puzzled and look on you as a crank. If you pursued the argument and compelled him to moralise his position, he would, I fancy, explain that the birds were very wicked creatures and that their cruelties to the worms and the insects were more than flesh and blood could stand. He would work himself up into a generous idealisation of himself as the guardian of law and order amid the bloody strife of the cabbage-patch—the preserver of the balance of nature. If cats were as clever as we, they would compile an atrocities blue-book about worms. Alas, poor thrush, with how bedraggled a reputation you would come through such an exposure! With how Hunnish a tread you would be depicted treading the lawn, sparing neither age nor sex, seizing the infant worm as it puts out its head to take its first bewildered peep at the rolling sun! Cats could write sonnets on such a theme. . . . Then there is that other beautiful potential poem, *The Cry of the Snail* . . . How tender-hearted cats are! Their sympathy seems to be all but universal, always on the look out for an object, ready to extend itself anywhere where it is needed, except, as is but human, to their victims. Yellow eyes or not, I begin to be persuaded that the cat next door is a noble fellow. It may well be that his look as I pass is a look not of fear but of repulsion. He has seen me going out among the worms with a sharp — no, not a very sharp — spade, and regards me as no better than an ogre. If I could only explain to him! But I shall never be able to do so. He could no more appreciate my point of view about worms than I can appreciate his about robins. Luckily, we both eat chicken. This may ultimately help us to understand one another.

On the other hand, part of the fascination of cats may be due to the fact that it is so difficult to come to an understanding with them. A man talks to a horse or a dog as to an equal. To a cat he has to be deferential as though it had some Sphinx-like quality that baffled him. He cannot order a cat about with the certainty of being obeyed. He cannot be sure that, if he speaks to it, it will even raise its eyes. If it is perfectly comfortable, it will not. A cat is obedient only when it is hungry or when it takes the fancy. It may be a parasite, but it is never a servant. The dog does your bidding,

but you do the cat's. At the same time, the
contrast between the cat and the dog has often
been exaggerated by dog-lovers. They tell
you stories of dogs that remained with their
dead masters, as though there were no fidelity
in cats. It was only the other day, however,
that the newspapers gave an account of a cat
that remained with the body of its murdered
mistress in the most faithful tradition of the
dogs. I know, again, of cats that will go out
for a walk with a human fellow-creature, as
dogs do. I have frequently seen a lady walking across Hampstead Heath with a cat in
train. When you go for a walk with a dog,
however, the dog protects you : when you go
for a walk with a cat, you feel that you are
protecting the cat. It is strange that the cat
should have imposed the myth of its helpless-
ness on us. It is an animal with an almost
boundless capacity for self-help. It can jump
up walls. It can climb trees. It can run, as
the proverb says, like "greased lightning."
It is armed like an African chief. Yet it has
contrived to make itself a pampered pet, so
that we are alarmed if it attempts to follow us
out of the gate into a world of dogs, and only

58

CATS

feel happy when it is purring—rolling on its back and purring as we rub its Adam's apple —by the fireside. There is nothing that gives a greater sense of comfort than the purring of a cat. It is the most flattering music in nature. One feels, as one listens, like a humble lover in a bad novel, who says : "You do, then, like me—a little—after all ?" The fact that a cat is not utterly miserable in our presence always comes with the freshness and delight of a surprise. The happiness of a crowing baby, newly introduced to us, may be still more flattering, but a cat will get round people who cannot tolerate babies.

It is all the more to be wondered at that a cat, which is such a master of this conversational sort of music, should ever attempt any other. There never was an animal less fit to be a singer. Someone—was it Cowper?—has said that there are no really ugly voices in nature, and that he could imagine that there was something to be said even for the donkey's bray. I should have thought that the beautiful voices in nature were few, and that most of them could be defended only on the ground of some pleasant association. Humanity, at least, has been unanimous in its condemnation of the cat as part of nature's chorus. Poems have been written in praise of the corncrake as a singer, but never of the cat. All the associations we have with cats have not accustomed us to that discordant howl. It converts love itself into a torment such as can be found only in the pages of a twentieth-century novel. In it we hear the jungle decadent—the beast in dissolution, but not yet civilised. When it rises at night outside the window, we always explain to visitors: " No; that's not Peter. That's the cat next door with the yellow eyes." The man who will not defend the honour of his cat cannot be trusted to defend anything.

VI

MAY

MAY is chiefly remarkable for being the only
month in which one does not like cats. June,
too, perhaps; but, after that, one does not
mind if the garden is full of cats. One likes
to have a wild beast whose movements, lazy
as those of Satan, will terrify the childish
birds out of the gooseberry bushes and the
raspberries and strawberries. He will not, we
know, have much chance of catching them as
late as that. They will be as cunning as he,
and the robin will wind his alarum-clock, the
starling in the plum-tree will cry out like a
hysterical drake, and the blackbird will make
as much noise as a farmyard. The cat can but
blink at the clamour of such a host of cunning
sentinels and, pretending that he had come
out only to take the air, return majestically to
his dinner of leavings in the kitchen. In May
and June, however, one does not wish the
birds to be frightened. One would like one's

garden to be an Alsatia for all their wings and all their songs. There is no hope of this in a garden full of cats. Even a Tetrazzini would cease to be able to produce her best trills if, every time she opened her mouth, a tiger padded in her direction down a path of currant bushes. There are, it may be admitted, heroic exceptions. The chaffinch sits in the plum and blusters out his music, cat or no cat. To be sure, he only sings, a flush of all the colours, in order to distract our attention. He is not an artist but a watchman. If you look into the buddleia-tree beside him, you will see his hen moving about in silence, creeping, dancing, fluttering, as she gorges herself with insects. She is a fly-catcher at this season, leaping into the air and pirouetting as she seizes her prey and returns to the bough. She is restless and is not content with the spoil of a single tree. She flings herself gracefully, like a ballet-dancer, into the plum, and takes up a caterpillar in her beak. She does not eat it at once, but stands still, eyeing you as though awaiting your applause. Her husband, sitting on the topmost spray, goes on singing his version of *The Roast Beef of Old England.*

MAY

She does not even now eat the caterpillar, but hurries along the paths of the branches with the obvious purpose of finding a tasty insect to eat along with it. It may be that there are insects that play the part of mustard or Worcestershire sauce in the chaffinch world. What a meal she is making in any case before she hurries back to her nest! It seems that among the chaffinches the male is the more spiritual of the sexes. But then he has so little to do compared with the female. He is still in that state of savagery in which the male dresses finely and idles.

The thrush cannot carry on with the same indifference to cats. He is the most nervous of parents, and spends half his time calling on his children to be careful. The young thrush hopping about on the lawn knows nothing of cats and refuses to believe that they are dangerous. He is not afraid even of human beings. His parent becomes argumentative to the point of tears, but the young one stays where he is and looks at you with a sideways jerk of his head as much as to say: "Listen to the old 'un." You, too, begin to be alarmed at such boldness. You know, like the pitiful parent, that the world is a very dangerous place, and that your neighbour's cat goes about like a roaring lion seeking whom he may devour. It has been contended by some men of science that all birds are born fearless after the manner of the young thrush, and that fear is a lesson that has to be taught to each new generation by the more experienced parents. Fear, they say, is not an inherited instinct, but a racial tradition that has to be communicated like the morality of civilised people. The young thrush on the lawn is certainly a witness on behalf of this theory. He hops towards you instead of away from you. He moves his gaping beak as though he were trying to say something. If there were no cats in the world, you would encourage his confidences, but you feel that, much as you would like to make friends with him, you must, for his own sake, give him his first lesson in fear. You try to give yourself the appearance of a grim giant : it has no effect on him. You make a quick movement to chase him away : he runs a few yards and then stops and looks round at you as though you were playing a game. It is too much to expect of you that you will actually throw stones at a bird for its

good, and so you give up his education as a
bad job. Alas, in two days, your worst fears
are justified. His dead body is found, torn
and ruffled, among the bushes. Some cat has
murdered him—murdered him, evidently, not
in hunger, but just for fun. Two indignant
children, one gold, one brown, discover the
dead body and bring in the tale. They
prepare the funeral rites of one whose only
sin was his innocence. This is not the first
burial in the garden. There is already a
cemetery marked with half-a-dozen crosses
and heaped with flowers under the pear-tree
on the south wall. Here is where the mouse
was buried; here where the starling; and
here the rabbit's skull. They all lie there
under the earth in boxes, as you and I will lie,
expecting the Last Trump. The robins are
not kinder to the "friendless bodies of un-
buried men" than are children to the bodies
of mice and birds. Here the ghost of no
creature haunts reproaching us with the
absence of a tomb, as the dead sailor washed
up on an alien shore reproaches us so often in
the pages of *The Greek Anthology*. There is a
procession to the grave and all due ceremony.

There is even a funeral service. Over the starling, perhaps, it lacked something in appropriateness. The buriers meant well, however. Their favourite in verse at the time was *Lars Porsena of Clusium*, and they gave the starling the best they knew—gave it to him from beginning to end. What he made of it, there is no telling: he is, it is said, an impressionable bird, though something of a satirist. Someone, overhearing them, recommended a briefer and more fitting service for the future. The young thrush had the benefit of the advice. He was laid to his last rest with the recitation of that noblest of valedictories: "Fear no more the heat o' the sun," over his tomb. He is now gone where there is no cat or parent to disturb. The priests who buried him declare that he has been turned into a golden nightingale, and that there must be no noise or romping in the garden for three days, as not till then will he have arrived safely at the Appleiades. That is the name they give to the Pleiades—the seven golden islands whither pass the souls of dead mice and birds and dolls and where Scarlatti lives and where you, too, may expect to go if

66

you please them. Even the black cat will probably go there—one's own black cat. But not
the neighbour's cat—the reddish-brown one—
thief, murderer and beast. It is the neighbour's
cat that makes one believe there is a hell.

Short is the memory of man, however.
Shorter the memory of children. There is no
gloom that can withstand May pouring itself
out in the deep blue of anchusa and the paler
blue of lupin, gushing out in the yellow of
laburnum, tossing like the tides in the wind.
One is gloomy, perhaps, when one looks at
the lettuces and sees how slow is their growth.
Watching a plant grow is like watching a
kettle boil. It seems to take æons. The
patience of gardeners always astonishes me.
Were gardening my profession, I should spend
half my time inventing schemes for making
plants grow up in a night like Jonah's gourd.
I should not mind about parsnips. A parsnip
might mature as slowly as an oak and live as long
for all I care. There is something, it may be, to
be said for parsnips, as there is something, it
may be, to be said for Mr Bonar Law. But I
do not know it. They do not even tempt the
slugs and the leather-jackets away from the

lettuces. There is nothing that puzzles one more in a friend than if he confesses to a taste for parsnips. Immediately, a gulf yawns deeper than could be caused by any confession of religious or moral eccentricity. One's sympathies instinctively close up like a sea-anemone touched by a child's finger. Yet people eat them. All that you and I know about them is that kind words do not butter them; but, if you go to Covent Garden at the right time of the year, you will undoubtedly find them being sold for food. Why should they make one gloomy, however, seeing that one has successfully excluded them from one's garden? Perhaps one is gloomy because of the reflection that there must be many other gardens in which they are growing. Gloom of this kind, however, is mere philanthropy. Turn your eyes, instead, to the strawberry-flowers and think of June. Consider the broad beans and the young peas safe amid their tall stakes. Consider even the spring onions. Is it any wonder that the chaffinch sings and the wren is operatic on the thither side of the garden wall? High in the air the swifts scream, as they rush here and there

68

after their prey, like polo teams galloping, pulling up, scrimmaging, turning, and off on the gallop again. The swift is an evil-looking bird, but playful. He has none of the grace of the swallow, for he cannot fold his wings, and he is black as a devil-worshipper. Still, he knows more of sport than most of the birds. I suspect that those rushing companions are not merely bent on food but have chosen out one individual insect for their pursuit like a ball in a game. Otherwise, why such excitement? There are billions of insects to be had for the mere asking. The fly-catcher knows this. He can spend an hour at a meal without ever flying more than ten yards from his bough. Still, one rejoices in the energy of the swift. One wishes the greenfinch had a little of it. The yellow splashes on his wings are undoubtedly delightful, but why will he perch so long in the acacia wailing like a sick cricket? And why did Wordsworth write a poem in praise of him? Probably he mistook some other bird for him. Poets are like that. Or perhaps he liked a noise like the voice of a sick cricket. One can never tell with Wordsworth. He had a cuckoo-clock.

VII

NEW YEAR PROPHECIES

SOME people are surprised at the daring with which compilers of prophetic almanacs forecast the details of the future. The most astonishing thing of all is that nearly everybody still regards the future as a mystery. As a matter of fact, we know a great deal about the future. We know that next year will contain 365 days. We know—and this is rather a tribute to our cleverness—that the year 1924 will contain 366 days, and even the exact point at which the extra day will slip in. Ask a savage to point you out the extra day in Leap Year, and he will be more hopelessly at a loss than a man looking for a needle in a haystack, but even the most ignorant Christian will pick it out at the right end of February as neatly and inevitably as a love-bird on a barrel-organ picking out a fortune. The art of prophecy has grown with civilisation. Prophets were regarded as

almost divine persons in the old days, but now
every man is his own Isaiah. I am the most
modest of the prophets, but even I venture to
foretell that there will be an annular eclipse
of the sun in the coming year on the 8th of
April, that it will begin at twenty-two minutes
to 8 A.M. at Liverpool, and that it will be
visible at Greenwich. What clairvoyant could
go further? Test my mantic gifts at any other
point and I doubt not I can satisfy you. Do
you want to know at what time there will be
high water at Aberdeen on the afternoon of
the 24th January? The answer is : "Thirteen
minutes past one." Do you want to know
when partridge shooting will begin? I do
not even need to reflect before giving the
answer : "The 1st of September." And so
I could go on, almost *ad infinitum*, filling in
the details of the year in advance. On the
1st of March, for instance, being St David's
Day, there will be a banquet at which Mr
Lloyd George will make a reference to hills,
mists, God, and a country called Wales. On
the 28th of March, being Easter Monday, there
will be a Bank Holiday. On the 24th of May,
being Empire Day, the majority of shops in

PLEASURES OF IGNORANCE

Regent Street will hang out Union Jacks, and school children will salute the flag at Abinger Hammer, Communists in various parts of London gnashing their teeth the while. On the 15th of June the anniversary of Magna Charta will fall and will pass without any disturbance. On the 12th of July Orangemen will dress up in sashes and listen to orators whose speeches will prove the hollowness of the old adage that you cannot serve both God and Mammon. On the same day, Lord Birkenhead will celebrate his forty-ninth birthday, showing that Gallopers are born not made. Need I continue, however? The year is obviously going to be a crowded one. It will, as I have said, contain 365 days and will come to an end at 12 P.M. on St Silvester's Day at the time of the new moon.

I have said enough, I think, to prove that one knows a great deal more about the future than is generally realised. There may be sceptics who doubt the virtue of my prophecies. If there be such, all I ask is that they should mark them well and verify each of them as its fulfilment falls due. The expense will be small. The most serious item will be the journey to Aberdeen to see the tide coming in on the 24th of January; but, by taking up a collection in Aberdeen, it should be possible to reduce one's net outlay by the better part of a shilling. On the whole, there never were prophecies easier to verify. I confidently challenge comparison between them and any prophecy made by any Cabinet Minister during the last five years. I even challenge comparison with the much more respectable prophecies contained in *Raphael's Prophetic Messenger.* Raphael at times strains our credulity. When he tells us, for instance, that on the 27th of April it is going to be "cold and frosty" and that on the 29th of April we shall see "high winds, storms and thunder," we feel that he is giving a free rein to his imagination and treating prophecy not as a science but as an art. That the 30th of April will be "showery" I agree, but how does he know that there will be "high wind and lightning" on the 21st of December? I am also somewhat puzzled as to the means by which he arrives at the conclusions set forth in his "every-day" guide for each day in the year. I can myself prophesy what you will do on each day, but I cannot, as he does, prophesy what you ought to do. This introduces an ethical element which is beyond my scope or horoscope. We need not quarrel with him when he dismisses the 1st of January as "an unimportant day," but when he bids us on the 2nd of January "court, marry, and deal with females," we may reasonably ask: "Why?" His advice for the 3rd is more acceptable. "Be careful," he says, "until 1 P.M., then seek work and push thy business." That is about the time of day one prefers to begin to "seek work"; would there were more days in the calendar like the 3rd of January. Some saint must have it in his keeping. On the 7th, however, it will be safer to abstain from work altogether. Raphael says: "A very unfortunate P.M. and evening for most purposes. Court and deal with females." Sunday, the 9th, is better. "Ask favours," he says, "in the P.M., and court." Though January is less than half gone, I confess I am getting a little breathless with so much courting. Raphael probably recognises this, and a note of caution creeps into his advice on the 13th, on which he bids us "court and marry in the morning, then be careful." By the 18th, however, he is his

74

old self again. "Court," he says cheerfully, "marry and ask favours and push ahead." Then come one rather careful day and two unfortunate ones, till on the 22nd, in a burst of exuberance, he offers us the day of our lives. "Deal with others," he exhorts us, "and push thy business, seek work, travel, court, marry, buy and speculate." I doubt if all this can be crowded into twenty-four hours outside *The Arabian Nights*. Besides, as a result of following Raphael's advice, we are already bigamists several times over, and have become sick of the sight of a Registry Office. By the end of the month even Raphael shows signs of being a little weary of his scarcely veiled incitements to Bluebeardism. For the 29th he advises: "Avoid females and be very careful," and for the 30th, which is a Sunday: "Avoid females and superiors." I should just about think so.

We need not follow Raphael through the rest of the year. It is enough to say that he keeps us busy courting, marrying, seeking work, being careful, travelling, speculating, pushing ahead, and avoiding females right down till the end of December. He occasionally varies his formula, as when on the 6th of April he bids us: " Do not quarrel. Be quiet," and when, on the 23rd of June, he advises: " Ask favours of females, and travel." On the whole, however, his recommendations leave us with a sense of the desperate monotony of human existence. It is no wonder the novelists find it so difficult to invent an original plot. Nothing seems to happen—even in the future—except the same old thing. It is all as monotonous as North, South, East and West. We turn with relief to the page on which Raphael tells us what are the best days on which to hire maidservants and to set turkeys. Our interest redoubles when we come on his advice to those about to kill pigs. " Do this," he says, " between eight and ten in the morning, and between the first quarter and full of the Moon ; the pigs will weigh more, and the flavour of the pork be improved." Then there are " Legal and Commercial Notes," one of which—" A bailiff must not break into a house, but he may enter by the chimney "—suggests a subject for a drawing by Mr George Morrow. The medical notes are equally worthy of consideration. On one page we are given a list of herbal remedies, and we are told how one disease can be cured by pouring boiling water on hay (upland hay being better than meadow hay) and applying it to the stomach. But Raphael is no crank, as we see in his suggestion for the treatment of influenza :

"If you think you have got an attack of influenza slip off to bed at once and take the whisky or brandy bottle with you, and don't be afraid of it, for alcohol is the best medicine you can take as it kills the germs in the blood. Do not wait until you are half dead—remember that a stitch in time saves nine, even with health."

Even on the subject of the care of children's teeth he makes it clear that, whoever may have come under the blight of Pussyfoot, it is not he :

"I believe a Committee is to be appointed to inquire into the failing eyesight and decaying teeth in children. I think I have already stated that these troubles were due to the excessive amount of sugar or sweetstuffs consumed. All sweet things cause an excessive

77

exudation of saliva from the gums, which affect and impair both the teeth and the eyesight, for, despite of what dentist and doctor may say, there is an intimate relation between the two. Dr Sims Wallace, the eminent lecturer on Dental Surgery, recommends *Beer* or dry *Champagne* as an excellent mouth wash. They are also pleasant to the throat and stomach!"

The reader is now in a position to estimate for himself the extent to which he can rely on Raphael's judgment, and to decide how far he will accept the horoscope Raphael has cast for Mr Lloyd George. On this he writes:

" This gentleman has figured so prominently in our national affairs for the last few years, that it may not be out of place if I give a few remarks on his horoscope. The time of his birth is stated to have been January 17th, 1863, 8h. 55m. A.M., but neither myself, nor other Astrologers, are satisfied with this hour. I think he was born some minutes sooner. At his birth the Sun was in exact Square to Jupiter, and also in Square to Mars, and Mars was in Opposition to Jupiter. These are very ominous and important aspects. The former denotes great extravagance, and waste of money, and the latter gives impetuosity, and danger to the person."

He then proceeds to give a "brief analysis" of Mr Lloyd George's horoscope:

"The Sun near Ascendant — self-praise, egotism, self-satisfaction, fondness for publicity and notoriety.

Venus and Mercury on Ascendant—fluency in speech, agreeableness, desire to please, fondness for Music, Arts, and Sciences.

Mars in 2nd, in Opposition to Jupiter, unfavourable for financial undertakings, extravagance, carelessness, and losses in speculation.

Uranus in 4th, trouble at end of life.

Jupiter in the 8th, benefit or help from marriage partner.

Moon near cusp of the 11th, many friends, especially females.

The Aspects denote—Sun Square Jupiter and Mars, recklessness in expenditure, public disapprobation, and an unfavourable and sudden ending to life.

Venus in Trine to Saturn, and Moon in Sextile to Jupiter—domestic relations of the

happiest description, and the wife a great
help."

I frankly doubt if any man can foretell the
future of Mr Lloyd George. No one knows
what he will say or do to-morrow. We know
what phrases he will use, but we do not know
on what side he will use them, or what he
will mean by them. All we know is that Sir
William Sutherland will say ditto.

Let us, then, return to safer fields of prophecy. What, really, is going to happen in
1921? I think I know. Human beings will
behave like bewildered sheep. They will be
chiefly notable for their lack of moral courage.
Good men will apologise for the deeds of bad
men, and bad men will do very much as they
please. Cruel and selfish faces will be seen
in every railway carriage and in every omnibus,
but readers of the respectable Press will refuse
to believe that there are any cruel people outside Germany and Russia. Not one but all
the Ten Commandments will be broken, and
turkeys will be eaten on Christmas Day. Men
will die of disease, violence, famine and old age,
and others will be born to take their place. In-

NEW YEAR PROPHECIES

tellectuals will be pretentious—mules solemnly trying to look like Derby winners. There will be a considerable amount of lying, injustice, and self-righteousness. Dogs will be fairly decent, but some of them will bite. Above all, the human conscience will survive. It will survive. It will continue to be the old still, small voice we know—as still and as small as it is possible to be without disappearing into silence and nothingness. And some of us will get a certain amusement out of it all, and will prefer life rather than death. We shall also go on puzzling ourselves as to what under the sun it all means. Not even a murderer will be without a friend or a pet dog or cat or bird. That is what 1921 will be like. That, at least, is as certain as the time of the high tide at Aberdeen on the 24th of January.

VIII

ON KNOWING THE DIFFERENCE

IT was only the other day that I came upon a full-grown man reading with something like rapture a little book — *Ships and Seafaring Shown to Children*. His rapture was modified, however, by the bitter reflection that he had already passed so great a part of his life without knowing the difference between a ship and a barque; and, as for sloops, yawls, cutters, ketches, and brigantines, they were simply the Russian alphabet to him. I sympathise with his regret. It was a noble day in one's childhood when one had learned the names of sailing-vessels, and, walking to the point of the harbour beyond the bathing-boxes, could correct the ignorance of a friend : "That's not a ship. That's a brig." To the boy from an inland town every vessel that sails is a ship. He feels he is being shown a new and bewildering world when he is told that the only ship that has the right to be called a ship is a vessel with three masts (at least), all of them square-rigged. When once he has learned his lesson, he finds an unaccustomed delight in wandering along the dirtiest coal-quay, and recognising the barques by the fact that only two of their three masts are square-rigged, and the brigs by the fact that they are square-rigged throughout—a sort of two-masted ships. Vessels have suddenly become as real to him in their differences as the different sorts of common birds. As for his feelings on the day on which he can tell for certain the upper fore topsail from the upper fore top-gallant sail, and either of these from the fore skysail, the crossjack, or the mizzen-royal, they are those of a man who has mastered a language and discovers himself, to his surprise, talking it fluently. The world of shipping has become articulate poetry to him instead of a monoton-ous abracadabra.

It is as though we can know nothing of a thing until we know its name. Can we be said to know what a pigeon is unless we know that it is a pigeon? We may have seen it again and again, with its bottle-shoulders and shining neck, sitting on the edge of a chimney-pot, and noted it as a bird with a full bosom and swift wings. But if we are not able to name it except vaguely as a "bird," we seem to be separated from it by an immense distance of ignorance. Learn that it is a pigeon, however, and immediately it rushes towards us across the distance, like something seen through a telescope. No doubt to the pigeon-fancier this would seem but the first lisping of knowledge, and he would not think much of our acquaintance with pigeons if we could not tell a carrier from a pouter. That is the charm of knowledge—it is merely a door into another sort of ignorance. There are always new differences to be discovered, new names to be learned, new individualities to be known, new classifications to be made. The world is so full of a number of things that no man with a grain of either poetry or the scientific spirit in him has any right to be bored, though he lived for a thousand years. Terror or tragedy may overwhelm him, but boredom never. The infinity of things forbids it. I once heard of a tipsy young artist who, on his way home on a beautiful night, had his attention called by a maudlin friend to the stars, where they twinkled like a million larks. He raised his eyes to the heavens, then shook his head. "There are too many of them," he complained wearily. It should be remembered, however, that he was drunk, and that he did not know astronomy. There could be too many stars only if they were all turned out on the same pattern, and made the same pattern on the sky. Fortunately, the universe is the creation not of a manufacturer but of an artist.

There is scarcely a subject that does not contain sufficient Asias of differences to keep an explorer happy for a lifetime. It would be easy to do nothing but chase butterflies all one's days. It is said that thirteen thousand species of butterflies have been already discovered, and it is suggested that there may be nearly twice as many that have so far escaped the naturalists. After so monstrous a figure, we are not surprised to learn that there are sixty-eight species of butterflies in Great Britain and Ireland. We should be astonished, however, had we not already expended our astonishment on the larger number. How many of us are there who could name even half-a-dozen varieties? We all know the tortoiseshell and the white and the blue — the little blue butterflies that flutter over the gold and red of the cornfields. But the average man does not even know by name such varieties as the Camberwell Beauty, the Dingy Skipper, the Pearl-bordered Fritillary, and the White-letter Hairstreak. As for the moth, are there not as many sorts of moths as there are words in a dictionary? Many men give all the pleasant hours of their lives to learning how to know the difference between one of them and another. One used to see these moth-hunters on windless nights in a Hampstead lane pursuing their quarry fantastically with nets in the light of the lamps. In pursuing moths, they pursue knowledge. This, they feel, is life at its most exciting, its most intense. They regard a man who does not know and is not interested in the difference between one moth and another as a man not yet thoroughly awakened from his pre-natal sleep. And, indeed, one could not conceive a more appalling sort of blank idiocy than the condition of a man who could not tell one thing from another in any department of life whatever. We would rather change lives with a jelly-fish than with such a man. This luxury of variety was not meant to be ignored. We throw ourselves into it with exhilaration as a swimmer plunges into the sea. There are few forms of happiness I know which are more enviable than that of those who have eyes for birds and flowers. How they rejoice on learning that, according to one theory, there are a hundred and three different species of brambles to be found in these islands! They would not have them fewer by a single one. It is extraordinarily pleasant even for one who is mainly ignorant of the flowers and their families to come on two or three varieties of one flower in the course of a country walk. As a boy, he is excited by the difference between the pin-headed and the thrum-headed primrose. As he grows older, he scans the roadside for little peeping things that to a lazy eye seem as like each other as two peas — the dove's foot geranium, the round-leaved geranium and the lesser wild geranium. "As like each other as two peas," we have said: but *are* two peas like each other? Who knows whether the peas have not the same differences of feature among themselves that Englishmen have?

PLEASURES OF IGNORANCE

Half the similarities we notice are only the results of our ignorance and idleness. The townsman passing a field of sheep finds it difficult to believe that the shepherd can distinguish between one and another of them with as much certainty as if they were his children. And do not most of us think of foreigners as beings who are all turned out as if on a pattern, like sheep? The further removed the foreigners are from us in race, the more they seem to us to be like each other. When we speak of negroes, we think of millions of people most of whom look exactly alike. We feel much the same about Chinamen and even Turks. Probably to a Chinaman all English children look exactly alike, and it may be that all Europeans seem to him to be as indistinguishable as sticks of barley-sugar. How many people think of Jews in this way! I have heard an Englishman expressing his wonder that Jewish parents should be able to pick out their own children in a crowd of Jewish boys and girls.

Thus our first generalisations spring from ignorance rather than from knowledge. They are true, so long as we know that they are not entirely true. As soon as we begin to accept them as absolute truths, they become lies. One of the perils of a great war is that it revives the passionate faith of the common man in generalisations. He begins to think that all Germans are much the same, or that all Americans are much the same, or that all Conscientious Objectors are much the same. In each case he imagines a lay figure rather than a human being. He may hate his lay figure or he may like it; but, if he is in search of truth, he had better throw the thing out of the window and try to think about a human being instead. I do not wish to deny the importance of generalisations. It is not possible to think or even to act without them. The generalisation that is founded on a knowledge of and a delight in the variety of things is the end of all science and poetry. Keats said that he sought the principle of beauty in all things, and poems are in a sense simply beautiful generalisations. They subject the unclassified and chaotic facts of life to the order of beauty. The mystic, meditating on the One and the Many, is also in pursuit of a generalisation—the perfect generalisation of the universe. And what is science but the attempt to arrange in a series of generalisations the facts of what we are vain enough to call the known world? To know the resemblances of things is even more important than to know the differences of things. Indeed, if we are not interested in the former, our pleasure in the latter is a mere scrap-book pleasure. If we are not interested in the latter, on the other hand, our sense of the former is apt to degenerate into guesswork and assertion and empty phrases. Shakespeare is greater than all the other poets because he, more than anybody else, knew how very like human beings are to each other and because he, more than anybody else, knew how very unlike human beings are to each other. He was master of the particular as well as of the universal. How much poorer the world would have been if he had not been so in regard not only to human beings but to the very flowers —if he had not been able to tell the difference between fennel and fumitory, between the violet and the gillyflower!

IX

THE INTELLECTUAL SIDE OF HORSE-RACING

HORSE-RACING—or, at least, betting—is one of the few crafts that are looked down on by practically everybody who does not take part in it. "It's a mug's game," people say. Even betting men talk like this. There is a street called Mug's Row in a north of England town: it is so called because the houses in it were built by a bookmaker. Whether it was the bookmaker or his victims that gave the street its name I do not know. To call a bookmaker a mug would seem to most people an abuse of language. Yet the only bookmaker I have ever really known used to confess himself a mug in the most penitent fashion. He was a mug, however, not because he could not make money, but because he could not keep it. The poor of his suburb, when in difficulties, he declared, used always to come to him instead of going to the clergy, and he was unable to refuse them. But then he was bitter against the clergy. As a young man, he had been a Sunday school teacher, and, so far as I could gather, he might have gone on being a Sunday school teacher till the present day if he had not suddenly been assailed with doubts one Sabbath afternoon as he expounded the story of David and Goliath. Whether it was that he looked on David as having taken an unsportsmanlike advantage of the giant or whether he doubted that so much could be done with such little stones, he did not make quite clear. Anyhow, from that day on, he never believed in revealed religion. He quarrelled with his clergyman. He broke the Sabbath. He began to drink beer and to go to race-meetings. He rapidly rose from the position of carpenter to that of bookmaker, and, were it not for his infernal gift of charity, he would probably now be driving his own car and be hall-marked with a Coalition title. Even as it was, he was much more prosperous than any carpenter. Whenever he produced money, it was in pocketfuls and handfuls. Strange that a bookmaker, who by his trade must be accustomed to miracles, should find

it difficult to believe in David and Goliath
He was possibly a man who betted on form,
and on form Goliath should undoubtedly have
won. David was an outsider. He had no
breeding. He would have been surprised if
he could have foreseen how his victory would
rankle some thousands of years later in the
soul of an honest English bookmaker.

It is, however, just these matters of form and
breeding that raise horse-racing and betting
above the intellectual level of a game of nap.
Betting men who ignore these things are as
unintellectual as the average novelist. There
are some, for instance, who shut their eyes
and bring down a pin or a pencil on a list
of names of the horses, in the hope that in
this way they may discover a winner. No
doubt they may. It is perhaps as good a way
as any other. But there is something trivial
in such methods. This is mere gambling for
the sake of excitement. There is no more
fundamental brainwork in it than in a game
I saw being played in a railway carriage the
other day, when a man drew a handful of
coins from his pocket and bet his friend half-
a-sovereign that there would be more heads

than tails lying uppermost. This is a game at which it is possible to lose five pounds in two minutes. It is the sort of game to which a betting man will resort when *in extremis,* but only then. The ruling passion is strong, however. I have a friend who on one occasion went into retreat in a Catholic monastery. Two well-known bookmakers had also gone into temporary retreat for the good of their souls. My friend told me that even during the religious services the bookmakers used to bet as to which of the monks would stand up first at the conclusion of a prayer, and that in the solemn hush of the worship he would suddenly hear a hoarse whisper: "Two to one on Brownie"—a brother with hair of that colour—and the answer: "I take you, Joe." I have even heard of men betting as to which of two raindrops on a window-pane will reach the bottom first. It is possible to bet on cats, rats or flies. Calvinists do not bet, because they believe that everything that happens is a certainty. The extreme betting man is no Calvinist, however. He believes that most things are accidents, and the rest catastrophes. Hence his philosophy is almost always that of

94

Epicurus. To him every day is a new day, at the end of which it is his aim to be able to say, like Horace, *Vixi*, or, as the text ought perhaps to read, *Vici*.

The intellectual betting man, on the other hand, has a position somewhere between the extremes of Calvinism and Epicureanism. He worships neither certainty nor chance. He reckons up probabilities. When Mr Asquith picked out Spion Kop as the winner of the Derby, he did so because he went about the business of selection not with a pin or a pencil, but with one of the best brains in England. In the course of his long conflicts with the House of Lords he had probably interested himself somewhat profoundly in questions of heredity and pedigree, and he was thus well equipped for an investigation into the records of the parentage and grandparentage of the various Derby horses. All that the ordinary casual better knows about Spion Kop is that he is the son of Spearmint, which won the Derby in 1906. This, however, would not alone make him an obviously better horse than Orpheus, whose sire, Orby, won the Derby in 1907. The student of breeding must be a feminist, who

95

pays as much attention to the female as to the
male line. It was by the study of the female
line that the most cunning of the sporting
journalists were able to eliminate Tetratema
from the list of probable winners. Tetratema,
as son of the Tetrarch, was excellently fathered
for staying the mile-and-a-half course at Epsom.
More than this, as a writer in *The Sportsman*
pointed out: "The Tetrarch himself is by Roi
Herode, a fine stayer, and his maternal grand-
dam was by Hagioscope, who rarely failed to
transmit stamina." It is when we turn to
Tetratema's mother, Scotch Gift—or is it his
grandmother something else?—apparently, that
we discover his hereditary vice. This mare our
journalist exposed to scathing and searching
criticism, and concluded that "there can be
nothing unreasonable in the inference, based
on the records of this family, that the chances
are against a Derby winner having descended
from the least distinguished of . . . four sisters."
Even so, however, the writer a few sentences
later abjures Calvinism, and denies that there
is anything certain in what he calls breeding
problems. "It seemed," he writes, "wildly
improbable at one time that Flying Duchess

would produce a Derby winner, for I believe it
is correct that two of Galopin's elder brothers
ran in a bus, and there were two others quite
useless. So, on the face of it, the chances
were against Galopin, the youngest brother."
I quote these passages as evidence of the immense demand the serious pursuit of horse-
racing puts on the intellect. The betting man
must be as well versed in precedents as a lawyer
and in genealogical trees as a historian. At
school, I always found the genealogical trees the
most difficult and bewildering part of history.
Yet the genealogical tree of a king is a simple
matter compared to that of a horse. All you
have to learn about a king is the names of his
relations : regarding a horse, however, you must
know not only the names but the character,
staying power and domestic virtues of every
male and female with whom he is connected
during several generations. If a man spent as
much labour in disentangling the cousinship of
the royal families of ancient Egypt, he would
be venerated as a scholar in five continents.
Oxford and Cambridge would shower degrees
on him. Sir William Sutherland would get him
a place on the Civil List. Hence it seems to

me that tipping the winners is not, as is too often regarded, " anybody's job " : it is work that should be undertaken only by men of powerful mind. No man should be allowed to qualify as a tipster unless he has taken a degree at one of the Universities. The ideal tipster would at once be a great historian, a great antiquary, a great zoologist, a great mathematician, and a man of profound common-sense. It is no accident that an ex-Prime Minister was one of the few Englishmen to spot the winner of the Derby of 1920. Mr Asquith must have gone patiently through all Spion Kop's relations, weighing up the chances whether it was an accident or owing to the weather that such an one fifteen years ago was beaten by a neck in a six-furlong race, studying incidents in every one of their careers, seeing that none of them had ever had a great-uncle a bus-horse, bringing out a table of logarithms to decide difficult points. . . . We need not be surprised that there are fewer great tipsters than great poets. Shakespeare alone has given us a portrait of the perfect tipster—"looking before and after . . . in apprehension how like a god !"

It is perhaps, however, when we leave questions of breeding and come to those of form, that we realise most fully the amazing intellectualism of the betting life. In the study of form we are faced by problems that can be solved only by the higher algebra. Thus, if Jehoshaphat, carrying 7 st., ran third to Jezebel, carrying 8 st. 4 lb., in a mile race, and Jezebel, carrying 8 st. 4 lb., was beaten by a neck by Woman and Wine, carrying 7 st. 9 lb., over a mile and a quarter, and Woman and Wine, carrying 8 st. 1 lb., was beaten by Tom Thumb, carrying 9 st. in a mile 120 yds., and Tom Thumb, carrying 9 st. 7 lb., was beaten by Jehoshaphat over seven furlongs, we have to calculate what chance Tom Thumb has of beating Jezebel in a race of a mile and a half on a wet day. There are men to whom such calculations may come easy. To Mr Asquith they are probably child's play. For myself, I shrink from them and, if I were a betting man, would no doubt in sheer desperation be driven back on the method of pin and pencil. But it is obvious that the sincere betting man has to make such calculations daily. Every morning the student of form finds his sporting page full of such lists as the following :—

PLEASURES OF IGNORANCE

0 0 0 CONCLUSIVE (7-5), Kroonstad—Conclusion.   8th of 9 to Poltava (gave 17lb.) Gatwick May (6f) and 7th of 19 to Orby's Pride (rec 4lb) Kempton May (5f).

3 3 3 RAPIERE (7-4), Sunder—Gourouli. Lost $\frac{3}{4}$ length and 3 lengths to Bantry (gave 2lb) and Marcia (rec 7lb) Newmarket May (1m), GOLDEN GUINEA (gave 20lb) not in first 9. See BLACK JESS.

0 0 4 ROYAL BLUE (7-0), Prince Palatine —China Blue.   See NORTHERN LIGHT.

0 2 0 BLACK JESS (6-11), Black Jester—Diving Bell.   Not in first 4 to St Corentin (gave 12lb) Lingfield last week (7f).   Here Ap. (7f) lost 3 lengths to Victory Speech (rec 1lb), RAPIERE (gave 13lb, favourite) $\frac{1}{2}$ length off.

0 LLAMA (6-11), Isard II. — Laughing Mirror.   Nowhere to Silver Jug (gave 15lb) Newbury Ap. (7f).

Is not a page of Thucydides simpler?   Is Persius himself more succinct or obscure?   Our teachers used to apologise for teaching us Latin grammar and mathematics by telling us that they were good mental gymnastics.   If education is only a matter of mental gymnastics,

however, I should recommend horse-racing as
an ideal study for young boys and girls. The
sole objection to it is that it is so engrossing ; it
might absorb the whole energies of the child.
The safety of Latin grammar lies in its dull-
ness. No child is tempted by it into forgetting
that there are other duties in life besides mental
gymnastics. Horse-racing, on the other hand,
comes into our lives with the effect of a religious
conversion. It is the greatest monopolist among
the pleasures. It affects men's conversation.
It affects their entire outlook. The betting
man's is a dedicated life. Even books have a
new meaning for him. *The Ring and the Book*
—it is his one and only epic. And it is the
most intellectual of epics. That is my point.

X

WHY WE HATE INSECTS

It has been said that the characteristic sound
of summer is the hum of insects, as the
characteristic sound of spring is the singing of
birds. It is all the more curious that the word
"insect" conveys to us an implication of ugliness. We think of spiders, of which many
people are more afraid than of Germans. We
think of bugs and fleas, which seem so in-
decent in their lives that they are made a jest
by the vulgar and the nice people do their
best to avoid mentioning them. We think
of blackbeetles scurrying into safety as the
kitchen light is suddenly turned on—blackbeetles which (so we are told) in the first
place are not beetles, and in the second place
are not black. There are some women who
will make a face at the mere name of any of
these creatures. Those of us who have never
felt this repulsion—at least, against spiders

and blackbeetles—cannot but wonder how far
it is natural. Is it born in certain people, or
is it acquired like the old-fashioned habit of
swooning and the fear of mice? The nearest
I have come to it is a feeling of disgust when
I have seen a cat retrieving a blackbeetle just
about to escape under a wall and making a dish
of it. There are also certain crawling creatures
which are so notoriously the children of filth
and so threatening in their touch that we
naturally shrink from them. Burns may make
merry over a louse crawling in a lady's hair,
but few of us can regard its kind with
equanimity even on the backs of swine. Men
of science deny that the louse is actually
engendered by dirt, but it undoubtedly thrives
on it. Our anger against the flea also arises from
the fact that we associate it with dirt. Donne
once wrote a poem to a lady who had been
bitten by the same flea as himself, arguing
that this was a good reason why she should
allow him to make love to her. It is, and
was bound to be, a dirty poem. Love, even of
the wandering and polygynous kind, does not
express itself in such images. Only while
under the dominion of the youthful heresy of

ugliness could a poet pretend that it did.
The flea, according to the authorities, is
"remarkable for its powers of leaping, and
nearly cosmopolitan." Even so, it has found
no place in the heart or fancy of man. There
have been men who were indifferent to fleas,
but there have been none who loved them,
though if my memory does not betray me,
there was a famous French prisoner some
years ago who beguiled the tedium of his cell
by making a pet and a performer of a flea.
For the world at large, the flea represents
merely hateful irritation. Mr W. B. Yeats
has introduced it into poetry in this sense in
an epigram addressed "to a poet who would
have me praise certain bad poets, imitators of
his and of mine":

You say as I have often given tongue
In praise of what another's said or sung,
'Twere politic to do the like by these,
But where's the wild dog that has praised his
     fleas?

When we think of the sufferings of human
beings and animals at the hands—if that is
the right word—of insects, we feel that it is
pardonable enough to make faces at creatures

WHY WE HATE INSECTS

so inconsiderate. But what strikes one as remarkable is that the insects that do man most harm are not those that horrify him most. A lady who will sit bravely while a wasp hangs in the air and inspects first her right and then her left temple will run a mile from a harmless spider. Another will remain collected (though murderous) in presence of a horse-fly, but will shudder at sight of a moth that is innocent of blood. Our fears, it is evident, do not march in all respects with our sense of physical danger. There are insects that make us feel that we are in presence of the uncanny. Many of us have this feeling about moths. Moths are the ghosts of the insect world. It may be the manner in which they flutter in unheralded out of the night that terrifies us. They seem to tap against our lighted windows as though the outer darkness had a message for us. And their persistence helps to terrify. They are more troublesome than a subject nation. They are more importunate than the importunate widow. But they are most terrifying of all if one suddenly sees their eyes blazing crimson as they catch the light. One thinks of nocturnal rites in an African forest temple and of terrible jewels blazing in the head of an evil goddess—jewels to be stolen, we realise, by a foolish white man, thereafter to be the object of a vendetta in a sensational novel. One feels that one's hair would be justified in standing on end, only that hair does not do such things. The sight of a moth's eye is, I fancy, a rare one for most people. It is a sight one can no more forget than a house on fire. Our feelings towards moths being what they are, it is all the more surprising that superstition should connect the moth so much less than the butterfly with the world of the dead. Who save a cabbage-grower has any feeling against butterflies? And yet in folk-lore it is to the butterfly rather than to the moth that is assigned the ghostly part. In Ireland they have a legend about a priest who had not believed that men had souls, but, on being converted, announced that a living thing would be seen soaring up from his body when he died—in proof that his earlier scepticism had been wrong. Sure enough, when he lay dead, a beautiful creature " with four snow-white wings " rose from his body and fluttered round his head. " And this," we are told, "was the first butterfly that was ever seen in Ireland; and now all men know that the butterflies are the souls of the dead waiting for the moment when they may enter Purgatory." In the Solomon Islands, they say, it used to be the custom, when a man was about to die, for him to announce that he was about to transmigrate into a butterfly or some other creature. The members of his family, on meeting a butterfly afterwards, would exclaim : "This is papa," and offer him a coco-nut. The members of an English family in like circumstances would probably say : "Have a banana." In certain tribes of Assam the dead are believed to return in the shape of butterflies or house-flies, and for this reason no one will kill them. On the other hand, in Westphalia the butterfly plays the part given to the scapegoat in other countries, and on St Peter's Day, in February, it is publicly expelled with rhyme and ritual. Elsewhere, as in Samoa—I do not know where I found all these facts—probably in *The Golden Bough*—the butterfly has been feared as a god, and to catch a butterfly was to run the risk of being struck dead. The moth, for all I know, may be the centre of as many legends, but I have not met them. It may be, however, that in many of the legends the moth and the butterfly are not very clearly distinguished. To most of us it seems easy enough to distinguish between them; the English butterfly can always be known, for instance, by his clubbed horns. But this distinction does not hold with regard to the entire world of butterflies—a world so populous and varied that thirteen thousand species have already been discovered, and entomologists hope one day to clasify twice as many more. Even in these islands, indeed, most of us do not judge a moth chiefly by its lack of clubbed horns. It is for us the thing that flies by night and eats holes in our clothes. We are not even afraid of it in all circumstances. Our terror is an indoors terror. We are on good terms with it in poetry, and play with the thought of

The desire of the moth for the star.

We remember that it is for the moths that the pallid jasmine smells so sweetly by night. There is no shudder in our minds when we read :

WHY WE HATE INSECTS

And when white moths were on the wing,
  And moth-like stars were flickering out,
I dropped the berry in a stream,
  And caught a little silver trout.

No man has ever sung of spiders or earwigs or
any other of our pet antipathies among the
insects like that. The moth is the only one
of the insects that fascinates us with both its
beauty and its terror.

I doubt if there have ever been greater
hordes of insects in this country than during
the past spring. It is the only complaint
one has to make against the sun. He is a
desperate breeder of insects. And he breeds
them not in families like a Christian but in
plagues. The thought of the insects alone
keeps us from envying the tropics their blue
skies and hot suns. Better the North Pole
than a plague of locusts. We fear the
tarantula and have no love for the tse-tse fly.
The insects of our own climate are bad enough
in all conscience. The grasshopper, they say,
is a murderer, and, though the earwig is a
perfect mother, other insects, such as the
burying-beetle, have the reputation of parri-
cides. But, dangerous or not, the insects are

for the most part teasers and destroyers. The greenfly makes its colonies in the rose, a purple fellow swarms under the leaves of the apples, and another scoundrel, black as the night, swarms over the beans. There are scarcely more diseases in the human body than there are kinds of insects in a single fruit tree. The apple that is rotten before it is ripe is an insect's victim, and, if the plums fall green and untimely in scores upon the ground, once more it is an insect that has been at work among them. Talk about German spies! Had German spies gone to the insect world for a lesson, they might not have been the inefficient bunglers they showed themselves to be. At the same time, most of us hate spies and insects for the same reason. We regard them as noxious creatures intruding where they have no right to be, preying upon us and giving us nothing but evil in return. Hence our ruthlessness. We say: "Vermin," and destroy them. To regard a human being as an insect is always the first step in treating him without remorse. It is a perilous attitude and in general is more likely to beget crime than justice. There has never, I believe,

been an empire built in which, at some stage
or other, a massacre of children among a
revolting population has not been excused on
the ground that " nits make lice." " Swat that
Bolshevik," no doubt, seems to many reaction-
aries as sanitary a counsel as " Swat that fly."
Even in regard to flies, however, most of us
can only swat with scruple. Hate flies as we
may, and wish them in perdition as we may,
we could not slowly pull them to pieces, wing
after wing and leg after leg, as thoughtless
children are said to do. Many of us cannot
endure to see them slowly done to death on
those long strips of sticky paper on which
the flies drag their legs and their lives out
—as it seems to me, a vile cruelty. A distinguished novelist has said that to watch flies
trying to tug their legs off the paper one after
another till they are twice their natural length
is one of his favourite amusements. I have
never found any difficulty in believing it of
him. It is an odd fact that considerateness,
if not actually kindness, to flies has been made
one of the tests of gentleness in popular
speech. How often has one heard it said in
praise of a dead man : " He wouldn't have

hurt a fly!" As for those who do hurt flies, we pillory them in history. We have never forgotten the cruelty of Domitian. "At the beginning of his reign," Suetonius tells us, "he used to spend hours in seclusion every day, doing nothing but catch flies and stab them with a keenly sharpened stylus. Consequently, when someone once asked whether anyone was in there with Cæsar, Vibius Crispus made the witty reply : ' Not even a fly.' " And just as most of us are on the side of the fly against Domitian, so are most of us on the side of the fly against the spider. We pity the fly as (if the image is permissible) the underdog. One of the most agonising of the minor dilemmas in which a too sensitive humanitarian ever finds himself is whether he should destroy a spider's web, and so, perhaps, starve the spider to death, or whether he should leave the web, and so connive at the death of a multitude of flies. I have long been content to leave Nature to her own ways in such matters. I cannot say that I like her in all her processes, but I am content to believe that this may be owing to my ignorance of some of the facts of the case. There are, on the other hand, two acts of destruction in Nature which leave me unprotesting and pleased. One of these occurs when a thrush eats a snail, banging the shell repeatedly against a stone. I have never thought of the incident from the snail's point of view. I find myself listening to the tap-tap of the shell on the stone as though it were music. I felt the same sort of mild thrill of pleasure the other day when I found a beautiful spotted ladybird squeezing itself between two apples and settling down to feed on some kind of aphides that were eating into the fruit. The ladybird, the butterfly, and the bee—who would put chains upon such creatures? These are insects that must have been in Eden before the snake. Beelzebub, the god of the other insects, had not yet any engendering power on the earth in those days, when all the flowers were as strange as insects and all the insects were as beautiful as flowers.

XI

VIRTUE

THERE is grave danger of a revival of virtue in this country. There are, I know, two kinds of virtue, and only one of them is a vice. Unfortunately, it is the latter a revival of which is threatened to-day. This is the virtue of the virtuously indignant. It is virtue that is not content merely to be virtuous to the glory of God. It has no patience with the simple beauty and goodness of the saints. Virtue, in the eyes of the virtuously indignant, is hardly worthy to be called virtue unless it goes about like a roaring lion seeking whom it may devour. Virtue, according to this view, is a detective, inquisitor, and flagellator of the vices— especially of the vices that are so unpopular that the mob may be easily persuaded to attack them. One of the chief differences between the two kinds of virtue, I fancy, is that while true virtue regards the mob-spirit as an enemy, simular virtue (if we may adopt

the Shakespearean phrase) looks to the mob as
its cousin and its ally. To be virtuous in the
latter sense is obviously as easy as hunting rats
or cats. Virtue of this kind is simply the
eternal huntsman in man's breast with eyes
aglint for a victim. It is Mr Murdstone's
virtue — the persecutor's virtue. It is the
virtue that warms the bosom of every man who
is more furious with his neighbour's sins than
with his own. If virtue is merely an inflam-
mation against our neighbour's sins, what man
on earth is so mean as to be incapable of it?
To be virtuous in this fashion is as easy as
lying. Those who abstain from it do so not
out of lack of heart, but from choice. We
have read of the popularity of the ducking-
stool in former days for women taken in
adultery. Savage mobs may have thought
that by putting their hearts into this amusement they were making up to virtue for the
long years of neglect to which, as individuals,
they had subjected her. They might not have
been virtue's lovers, but at least they could be
virtue's bullies. After all, virtue itself is no
bad sport, when chasing, kicking, thumping,
and yelling are made the chief part of the

game. Sending dogs coursing after a hare is nothing to it. Man's enjoyment of the chase never rises to the finest point of ecstasy save when his victim is a human being. Man's inhumanity to man, says the poet, makes countless thousands mourn. But think also of the countless thousands that it makes rejoice! We should always remember that the Crucifixion was an exceedingly popular event, and in no quarter more so than among the virtuously indignant. It would probably never have taken place had it not been for the close alliance between the virtuously indignant and the mob.

To be fair to the virtuously indignant and the mob, they do not insist beyond reason that their victim shall be a bad man. Good hunting may be had even among the saints, and who does not enjoy the spectacle of a citizen distinguished mainly for his unblemished character being dragged down into the dust? We have no reason to believe that the people who were burned during the Inquisition were worse than their neighbours, yet the mob, we are told, used to gather enthusiastically and dance round the flames. The destructive instincts of the mob are such that in certain moods it is ready to destroy any kind of man, just as the destructive instincts of a puppy are such that in certain moods it is ready to destroy any sort of book—whether Smiles's *Self-Help* or *Mademoiselle de Maupin* is a matter of perfect indifference. The virtuously indignant maintain their power by constantly inciting and feeding this appetite for destruction. Hence, when we feel virtuously indignant, we would do well to inquire of ourselves if that is the limit and Z of our virtue. Have we no sins of our own to amend that we have all this time for barking and biting at the vices of our neighbours? And if we must attack the sins of our fellows, would it not be the more heroic course to begin with those we are most tempted by, instead of those to which we have no mind? Do not let the drunkard feel virtuous because he is able with an undivided heart to denounce simony, and do not let the forger, who happens to be a teetotaller because of the weakness of his stomach, be too virtuously indignant at the red-nosed patron of the four-ale bar. Any of us can achieve virtue, if by virtue we merely mean the avoidance of the vices that do not attract us. Most of us can boast than we have never been cruel to a hippopotamus or had dealings with a succubus or taken a bribe of a million pounds to betray a friend. On these points we can look forward with perfect confidence to the scrutiny of the Day of Judgment. I fear, however, the Recording Angel is likely to devote such little space as he can afford to each of us to the vices we have rather than to the vices we have not. Even Charles Peace would have been acquitted if he had been accused of brawling in church instead of murder. Hence it is to be hoped that passengers in railway trains will not remain content with gloating down upon the unappetising sins of which the forty-seven thousand are accused by Mr Pemberton Billing. Steep and perilous is the ascent of virtue, and the British public may well be grateful to Mr Billing and Mr Bottomley if they help it with voice or outstretched hand to climb to the snowy summits. So far as can be seen, however, all that Mr Billing and Mr Bottomley do is to interrupt the British public in its upward climb and orate to it on the monstrous vices of the Cities of the Plain.

VIRTUE

This may be an agreeable diversion for weary men, but it obviously involves the neglect of virtue, not the pursuit of it. Most people imagine that to pursue vice is to pursue virtue. But the wisdom of the ages tells us that the only thing to do to vice is to fly from it. Lot's wife was a lady who looked round once too often to see what was happening to the forty-seven thousand. Let Mr Billing and Mr Bottomley beware. Their interest in the Cities of the Plain will turn them into pillars of salt a thousand years before it turns them into pillars of society.

As for virtue, then, how is it to be achieved? Merely by blackening the rest of the world, we cannot hope to make ourselves white. Modern writers tell us that we cannot make ourselves white even by blackening ourselves. They denounce the sense of sin as a sin, and tell us that there is nothing of which we should repent except repentance. We need not stay to discuss this point. We know well enough that, so long as the human intellect (to leave the human conscience out of the question) survives, men will be burdened with the sense of imperfection and think enviously of the nobility of Epaminondas or Julius Cæsar or St Francis of Assisi. For we have to count even Julius Cæsar among the virtuous, though the scandalmongers would not have it so. His vices may have made him bald and brought about his assassination. But he had the heroic virtues—courage and generosity and freedom from vindictiveness. When we read how he wept at the death of his great enemy, and how "from the man who brought him Pompey's head he turned away with loathing, as from an assassin," we bow before the nobility of his character and realise that he was something more than a stern man and an adulterer. Pompey, too, had this gift of virtue — this capacity for turning away from foul means of besting his enemies. When he had captured Perpenna in Spain, the latter offered him a magnificent story of a plot, the knowledge of which would have put the lives of many leading Romans in his power. "Perpenna, who had come into possession of the papers of Sertorius, offered," says Plutarch, "to produce letters from the chief men of Rome, who had desired to subvert the existing order and change the form of government, and had

therefore invited Sertorius into Italy. Pompey,
therefore, fearing that this might stir up
greater wars than those now ended, put
Perpenna to death and burned the letters
without even reading them." It was hard on
Perpenna, but in burning the letters at least
Pompey gave us an example of virtue. It is
Plutarch's feeling for the beauty of such noble
actions that has made his biographies a primer
of virtue for all time. None of his heroes are
primarily "good" men. There is scarcely one
of them who could have been canonised by
any Church. They have enough of the weak-
nesses of flesh and blood to satisfy even the
most exacting novelist of these days. On the
other hand, they nearly all had that capacity
for grandeur of conduct which distinguishes
the noble man from the base. Plutarch never
pretends that mean and filthy motives and
generous motives do not jostle one another
strangely in the same breast, but his portraits
of great men give us the feeling that we are
in presence of men redeemed by their virtues
rather than utterly destroyed by their vices.
Suetonius, on the other hand, is the historian
of the forty-seven thousand. His book may

be recommended as scandalmongering—hardly as an aid to virtue. Here we have the servants' evidence of Roman history, the plots and the secret vices. Suetonius, fortunately, has the grace not to write as though in narrating his story of vice he were performing a virtuous act. If we are to have stories of fashionable sinners, let us at least have them naked and not dressed up in the language of outraged virtue. Scandal is sufficiently entertaining by itself. There is no need to lace it with self-righteousness.

XII

JUNE

THERE is always a cuckoo that stays out later than the other cuckoos. . . .

Two goldfinches came and sang in the catalpa-tree in the garden. . . .

It is difficult to decide with which sentence to begin. There are so many pleasures. The goldfinches have not come back again, however. They and the faint blue flowers of the catalpa turned a sinister growth for an interval into a small Paradise of colour and song. Then the flowers fell. They had no more life than snow in May. Coming as they did at the end of years of barrenness, they astonished one like the blossoming of the Rose of Sharon. But now the bough is dark and sinister and melancholy again. Sparrows squabble over their love affairs in it. The cuckoo that stays out later than the other cuckoos is the triumphant survivor.

PLEASURES OF IGNORANCE

Not that there is much to be said even for him as a model of continuance. His note will soon change. He will become hoarse and only half-articulate. He will cease to be the flying echo of the mystery of skies and woods at dawn and in the still evening. The disreputable bat, whose little wings flutter half visibly like waves of heat rising above a stove, will outlast him.

There is no getting beyond the old image of things in general as a stream that disappears. The flowers and the birds come in tides that sweep over the world and in a moment are lost like a broken wave. The lilacs filled with purple; laburnum followed, and in a few days all the gold ebbed, and nothing was left but a drift of withered blossoms on the ground; then came the acacia-flowers, white as the morning among the cool green plumage of the tree, and now they, too, have been turned into dirtiness and deserted foam. And in the hedges change has been as swift, as merciless—change so imperceptible in what it is doing, so manifest in what it has done. The white blossoms of the sloe gave place to the foam of the hawthorn

and the flat clusters of the wayfaring-tree;
now in its turn has come the flood of the
elder-flowers, a flood of commonness, and June
on the roads would hardly be beautiful were
it not for the roses that settle, delicate and
fleeting as butterflies, on the long and crooked
briers. Perhaps one has not the right to say
of any flower or any bird that it is not beautiful. Even elder-flowers, seen at a distance,
can give cheerfulness to a roadside. But, if
we have to pick and choose among flowers,
there are many who will give the lowest prize
to the flowers that have been compared to
umbrellas—elder-flowers, cow's parsley, hem-
lock, and the rest. These are the plebeians of
the hedges and ditches. They have the air
of something useful. One would imagine
they were intended to be cooked and eaten in
cheap restaurants. We experience no lifting
of the heart at sight of them. We should be
surprised to hear the abrupt ecstasy of a wren
issuing from among their leaves. And yet it
is hardly a week since, walking in a Sussex
lane, I saw a long procession of cow's parsley
on the top of a high bank silhouetted against
the twilight sky. There seemed never to

have been more exquisite flowers. They had captured the silver of evening as in a net.

There are many flowers that seem ugly to an indifferent eye. Even the red valerian, that sprouts so boldly in bushes of coral from the top of the wall, is regarded by some people as a weed and an impudent intruder. For myself, I love the spectacle of stone walls breaking out into flower with red valerian and ivy-leaved toad-flax. The country people have greeted these flowers with comic and friendly names. Valerian they call " drunken sailor," and the ivy-leaved toad-flax that blossoms in a thousand tiny blue butterflies from the stones has (so prolific it is) been given the nickname of " mother of thousands." I doubt, however, whether the country people have as many fanciful names for the flowers as they are represented as having in the books. When Mr W. H. Hudson first came on winter heliotrope in Cornwall, and was attracted by its meadow-sweet smell at a season when there were few other flowers, he was told by a countryman that it was called simply " weed." Countrymen, if they are asked the name of a flower, will often say that they do

not know, but that they call it so-and-so. A
small boy who was gathering green-stuffs for
his rabbits came up and walked beside me the
other day, and, on being shown some goose-
grass, and asked what name he knew it by,
said: "I don't know its name; we calls it
'cleavers.'" In my childhood, I never heard
it called by any other name than "robin-run-
the-hedge," and under that name alone am I
attracted by it. "Cleavers" is too reminiscent
of a butcher's yard or of some dull tool.
"Goose-grass" at least fills the imagination
with the picture of a bird. But "robin-run-
the-hedge" is better, for it is an image of wild
adventure. It will be a pity if the tradition
of picturesque names for flowers is allowed to
die. The kidney-vetch, a long yellow claw of
a flower that looks withered even at birth,
may not deserve a prettier name, but at least
it is possible to give it an ugly name with
more interesting associations. "Staunch" is
an older name that reminds us that the flower
was, a few generations ago, used to staunch
wounds. The other name, it is suggested,
had its origin in the supposed excellence of
the plant in curing diseases of the kidney.

PLEASURES OF IGNORANCE

But there seem to be no grounds for believing this. There are, unfortunately, some beautiful flowers for which no beautiful or even expressive name has ever been invented. Who is there who, coming on the blue scabious on a hill near the sea, is not conscious of the gross failure of the human race in never having found anything but this name out of a dustbin for one of the most charming of flowers? Matthew Arnold, appalled by some of the names of human beings that still flourished in the days of Victoria, and may for all I know be flourishing to-day, once hoped to turn us into Hellenists by declaring that there was "no Wragg on the Ilissus." Was there no "scabious" on the Ilissus either, I wonder? Were I a flower of the field, I should prefer to be called "nose-bleed" or "sow-thistle." On the whole, however, the plants have little to complain of in the matter of names. The milkwort that has been scattering its fine, delicate colours among the short grasses of the bare hills deserves its beautiful name, "grace of God." We think of it as the sprigging of a divine mantle cast over the June world. The greater plantain, that after

the recent rain has come out on the hills, with
a ruff of purple feathers round its brown cone,
neither deserves nor possesses a name con-
noting sacredness.   It is interesting mainly as
a plant that somehow became associated with
the voyages and travels of Englishmen, and is
known in America as "Englishman's foot,"
because, wherever the Englishman goes, the
plant follows him.

The riot of the spring flowers is already
passing, however.   As we walk along the path
through the corn, we find the wild mustard,
that a few weeks ago made a steep field blaze
like a precinct of the sun, already withering
into a mass of green pods ; and the hay in the
valley has been cut down with all its crimson
clover.   The smell of the tossed hay, as we
pass, sends back the memory into an older
world.   How is it that sweet smells do not
please us so much for what they are as for
the things of which they remind us ?   At the
smell of hay newly stacked we cease to be our
present age ; we are in a world as distant as
that of Theocritus.   There is no ambition in
it, no tears or taxes, no men and women
pretending, nothing that is not happy.   Every

scent is sweet, every sound is a laugh or a bird's song. Every man and woman and animal we behold is more interesting than if they had come out of a Noah's Ark. Smell has been described as the most sensual of the senses. It may be so, but it is surely also the sense that is most closely related to the memory. Old landscapes, old happinesses, old gardens, old people, come to life again —at times, almost unbearably so—with the smell of wallflower or hay or the sea. It may be, however, that this is not a universal experience. Some of us, no doubt, live more in our memories than others : it is our doom.

Even we, however, are sensualists of the open air, and the spectacle of the wind foaming among the leaves of the oak and elm can easily make us forget all but the present. The blue hills in the distance when rain is about, the grey arras of wet that advances over the plain, the whitethroat that sings or rather scolds above the hedge as he dances on the wing, the tree-pipit—or is it another bird ? —that sinks down to the juniper-tip through a honey of music, a rough sea seen in the

distance, half shine, half scowl—any of these
things may easily cut us off from history and
from hope and immure us in the present hour.
Or may they? Or do these things too not
leave us home-sick, discontented, gloomy—
gloomy if it is only because we are not nearly
so gloomy as we ought to be?

XIII

ON FEELING GAY

GAIETY has come back at least to parts of London. There never were greater crowds of people eating with bottles at their sides in public places. On the whole, however, there has been little down-heartedness at the restaurants during the past four and a half years. Even while the housewife in the red-brick street was wasting her mornings in the patient vigil of the queue, only to find at the end of it that there was no butter, no lard, no tea, no jam, no golden syrup, no prunes, no potatoes, no currants, no olive oil, or whatever it might be she wanted most, the restaurants never shut their doors as the grocers' shops and the confectioners' sometimes did. When rationing came, one could eat the greater part of the week's beef allowance at a single meal in the home, but in a restaurant one could get four excellent meat meals—in some restaurants even eight excellent meals—in return for a

week's coupons. There were, no doubt, parts
of the country in which the housewife was
hardly more restricted than the diner-out in
restaurants. Travellers came back from places
in Dorsetshire, Gloucestershire, and Scotland,
as from Ireland, with gorgeous narratives of
areas in which the King's writ did not run so
far as coupons were concerned and beef was
free if only you paid for it. But in London,
and especially in the Home Counties, there
was no such reign of liberty. The housewife
went shopping, as it were, on ticket-of-leave,
and even the sleepiest suburbans began to
realise that the arrival of our daily bread is a
daily miracle instead of the commonplace it
once seemed to be. Had Dr Faustus come
back to life a modern lady would have invoked
the aid of his magic for some food less romantic
than grapes out of season : she would have been
content with a tin of golden syrup. As for
butter, it is surprising that no one wrote a
sonnet to butter during the war. I have seen
eyes positively moisten with love at the sight of
a small dish of it. Even from the restaurants it
seemed to vanish for a time, and some of them
are still doing their best to help one to deceive

oneself with a curl of what is called butter substitute. The restaurant, however, seems to be better supplied than the home with the three great aids to gaiety—wine, jam and currants. I confess I have never been able to understand why currants should be generally regarded as one of the necessary ingredients of perfect pleasure. But they unquestionably are. The child on a holiday will eat a bun with only three currants in it with three times more pleasure than he will eat a frankly plain bun. A suet pudding without currants or raisins is prison fare, barren to the eye and cheerless: let but an infrequent currant or raisin peep from the mass and it is a pudding for a birthday. So universal is the passion for currants as an aid to pleasure that during the past three weeks the only matter that rivalled in general interest the question whether the Kaiser was to be hanged was the question whether we should have currants before Christmas. So profound is the disappointment of the public at the non-arrival of the currants that explanations have been put in the papers, calling on us to practise the sublime virtue of self-sacrifice, happy in the knowledge that all the currants are needed for invalid soldiers. But if the currants are needed for soldiers, how comes it that we sometimes find them in the puddings in restaurants? Those who are concerned for the preservation of home life in this country cannot but be perturbed by the way in which in this matter of currants the scales have been weighted in favour of the restaurant and against the home. As for jam, the diner in the restaurant rejoices in jam roll while the child in the home labours its way through tapioca pudding. Is it any wonder if, as the pessimists believe, the English home decays?

Whether as a result of the jam roll or the rare currants in the puddings, it has been unusually difficult to get a table at some of the restaurants since the signing of the Armistice. No doubt the signing of the Armistice itself had something to do with it. Christian men, whenever anything epoch - making happens, must have something to eat. Marriage, the return of a conquering hero, the visit of a great statesman, the birth of Christ—we find in all these things a reason for calling on the cooks to do their damnedest. Even the dyspeptic forgets his doctor's orders in the general

excitement and chases oysters down the narrow
stairway of his throat with thick soup, follows
thick soup with lobster, and lobster with turkey,
and turkey with a savoury, and the savoury with
a *pêche Melba,* and at the end of it will not reject
cheese and a banana, all of this accompanied
with streams of liquid in the form of wine,
coffee and brandy. I have often wondered why
a man should feel gay doing violence to his
entrails in this fashion. I have noticed again
and again that he loses a little of his gaiety if
the dinner is served slowly enough to give him
time to think. The gay meal, like the farce,
must be enacted quickly. The very spectacle
of waiters hurrying to and fro with an air of
peril to the dishes quickens the fancy, and the
gastric juices flow to an anapæstic measure.
Who does not know what it is to sit through
a slow meal and digest in spondees? One is
given time between the courses to turn philo-
sopher—to meditate becoming a hermit and
dining on a bowl of rice in a cave. Nothing
can prevent one from there and then coming
to a decision on the matter save a waiter with
the eye of a psychoanalyst ready to rush forward at the first sadness of an eyelid and tempt

one either with a new dish or with a glass
refilled. "Stay me with flagons; comfort me
with apples." It is a universal cry. Our desire
is for the banqueting-house. Perhaps it is not
so much that we feel gay as that we are afraid
of feeling gloomy. We have no force within
us that will enable us to laugh over a lettuce
and become wits on water. There must be an
element of riot in our eating and drinking if
we are to drive dull care away. That is the
defence of cakes and ale. Cakes, no doubt,
are not what they used to be, and ale is even
less so. But human beings are symbolists, and,
if you give them something that looks like cakes
and something that looks like beer, it is surprising how content they will be. Our eating
and drinking is but a game, and we deceive
ourselves at table like children among their
toys. Even the vegetarian lies his food into
grandeur not its own. There is a vegetarian
restaurant in London in which one of the
dishes on the bill of fare bears the name " Like
chicken." *Splendide mendax !*

One of the most amazing features in the
appearance of London at the present time is
surely the absence of the signs of widespread

mourning. The windows of the shops are full of all the colours of the parrot. The hats are as bright as a scrap-book. The confectioners' shops are making a desperate effort to look as if nothing had happened. The death of a single monarch would have darkened Christmas in Regent Street more effectually than the million mournings of the war. It is as though we were eager to conceal from ourselves the news of this terrible disaster. After all, to judge by the crowds in the streets, most people still remain alive. We have sworn we will never forget those others, but one has only to read some of the election speeches to see that with many of us our own greed and vindictiveness are already ousting the ideals for which hundreds of thousands of men gave up their lives. Can it be that we are feeling gay not only because we have escaped from the disasters of the war but because we are escaping from the ideals of the war? It is as though we had returned from the barren snows of the mountain-tops to the cosy plenty of the valleys. We are glad to exchange the stars as companions for the nearer illuminations of the streets. The familiar world is coming back, and civilian youths have begun

once more to sing music-hall choruses on the
way home on the tops of buses :—

> So I dillied,
> And dallied,
> And dallied,
> And dillied ;
> But you can't trust a speshul
> Like an old-time copper
> When you can't find your way home.

Peace had returned without question when
nonsense of this venerable kind sped into the
air from the roof of a late bus.   Well, we have
always wanted the world to be " as usual."   We
were angry with the Germans for plunging us
into the unusualness of war, and we feel scarcely
more friendly to those who would plunge us into
the unusualness of Utopia.   We feel at home
among neither horrors nor ideals.   We are glad
at the prospect of having the old world back
rather than at having to make a new world.
Lord Birkenhead, I observe, declares that it
would be an awful thing if the war had left us
unchanged, but we look in vain for signs of any
deep change even in the speeches of Lord
Birkenhead.   One noticeable change the war
has unquestionably made : more women smoke

in the restaurants than formerly. Sanguine people declare that other changes are impending; but other people, equally sanguine, are doing their best to prevent this. The human race is gradually feeling its way back to its traditional division into those who desire a change and those who desire to keep things as they are. The Christmas festival appeals to both equally. It is at once an old custom and the prophecy of a new earth. On such a day one can rejoice even without currants or the League of Nations. The world is a good place. Let us eat, drink, and be merry.

XIV

IN THE TRAIN

IT is said that travelling by train is to be made
still more uncomfortable. I doubt if there is
a man of sufficient genius in the Government
to accomplish this. Are not the trains already
merely elongated buses without the racing
instincts of the bus? Have they not already
learned to crawl past mile after mile of back-
yard and back garden at such a snail's pace
that we have come to know like an old friend
every disreputable garment hung out on the
clothes-lines of a score of suburbs? Do they
not stand still at the most unreasonable places
with the obstinacy of an ass? Stations, the
names of which used to be an indistinguishable
blur as we swept past them as on a swallow's
wing, have now become a part of the known
world, and have as much attention paid to them
as though they were Paris or Vienna. Equality
has not yet been established among men, but
it has been established among stations. There
never was such a democracy of frightfulness.

PLEASURES OF IGNORANCE

We seldom see a station which has about it the air of permanence. There are, I believe, good historical reasons why there are no Tudor stations or Queen Anne stations to be found in the country. Still, I know of no reason why so many stations should look as though they had been built hurriedly to serve the needs of a month, like a travelling show in a piece of waste ground. Not that the railway station has any of the gaudy detail of the travelling show. It resembles it only in its dusty and haphazard setting. It is more like a builder's or a tombstone-maker's yard. The very letters in which the name of the station is printed are often of a deliberate ugliness. No newspaper would tolerate letters of such an ugliness in its headlines. They stare at one vacuously, joylessly. It is said that the village of Amberley is known to the natives as "Amberley, God help us!" How many stations look at us from their name-plates with that "God help us!" air! What I should like to see would be a name-plate that would seem to announce to us in passing: "Glasgow, thank God!" or whatever the name of the station may be. I have never yet discovered a merry station. Here

and there a station-master has done his best
to make the place attractive by planting gera-
niums in the form of letters to spell the name
of the place on a neighbouring embankment.
But these things remind one of the flowers on a
grave. And the people who walk up and down
the platform, their noses cold in the wind, are
hardly more cheerful than undertakers' men.
Even the porters in their green trousers, who
roll the milk-cans along the platform to the
luggage-van with an energy and a clatter that
would satisfy the ambition of any healthy
child, do not look merry. There was one
cheerful porter who used to welcome you like
a host, and make a jest as he clipped your
railway ticket—"Just to lighten your load,
sir!"—but the Government had him removed
and put to mind gates at a crossing where he
would not be able to speak to the passengers.
As a rule, however, nobody looks as if he
liked being in a railway station or would stop
there if he could go anywhere else. I trust
the Ministry of Reconstruction will see to it
that the railway stations of the country are
rebuilt and vivified. One does not really wish
to stop at any station at all except one's own

station. But if one has to do so, let the stations be made more amusing.

Unfortunately, it is not only the frequent stops that have made railway travelling almost ideally uncomfortable. The Government seems also to have hired a staff of workers to impregnate the seats of the carriages with dust and to scatter all the dust that can be spared in these exiguous days on the floors. They have also a gang of old and wheezy gentlemen who travel up and down the line all day shutting the windows. This work is sometimes deputed to women. They are forbidden to say " May I ? " or " Do you mind ? " or to make use of any civil expression that might mollify the traveller sitting by the window. It is part of their instructions to reach past him with an air of independence and to have the window shut and the book that he is reading knocked out of his hand before he has time to see what has happened. Some day someone will write a book about the alteration of English manners that took place during the Great War. I believe the alteration is largely due to these Government hirelings whose duty it is to make railway travel a burden

and never to say " Please " or " Thank
you."

Even now, however, there are compensations.
In the morning the shadows are long, and, as
one rattles north among the water-meadows,
the flying plumes of the engine leave a procession of melting silhouettes on the fields to
the west. Rooks oar their way towards their
homes with long twigs in their beaks. Horses
go through the last days of their kingship
dragging ploughs and harrows over the fields
with slow and monotonous tread. Here a hill
has been ploughed into a sea of little brown
waves. Further on a meadow is already bright
with the green of winter-sown corn. The
country has never been so laboured before.
Chalk and sand and brown earth and red are
all being turned up and broken and bathed in
the sun and wind. Adam has begun to delve
again. There is the urgency of life in fields
long idle. It is not that the fields have become
populous. One sees many laboured fields, but
little labour. The occasional plough-horse,.
however, brings strength into the stillness.
How noble a figure of energy he makes !

As for us who sit in the railway train, we do

not look at him much. We are all either
reading papers or talking. Two old men,
bearded and greasy-coated, tramps of a bygone
era, sit opposite one another and neither read
nor talk. One of them is blear-eyed and
coughs, and has an unclean moustache. All
his friend ever says to him is: "Clean your
nose," making an impatient gesture. A young
man in a bowler hat and spectacles, who smokes
a pipe in inward-drawn lips, discusses the
Labour situation with some acquaintances.
"They would be all right," he explains, "if it
wasn't for the Labour leaders. You know what
a Labour leader is. He's a chap that never did
an honest day's work in his life. He finds it
pays better to jaw than to work, and I don't
blame him. After all, it's human nature.
Every man's out to do the best for himself,
isn't he?" "Your nose—blow your nose,"
mumbled the tramp across the carriage.
"Take Australia," continues the young man;
"they've had Labour Governments in Australia.
What good did they do for the working man?
Did they satisfy him? Why, there were more
strikes in Australia under the Labour Government than there ever had been before." "Did

you hear that, Johnny?" I heard another voice saying. "A tame rabbit was sold Sat'day in Guildford market for twelve-and-sixpence!" "How did they know it was a tame one?" "Ah, now you're asking!" A man looked up from *The Morning Post* with interest in his face. "Why," he said, "is a tame rabbit considered to be better eating than a wild one?" It was explained to him that wild rabbits were often kept for a long time after they were killed, and were therefore regarded as more dangerous. Otherwise, the tame rabbit had no point of superiority. "What do *you* say, Johnny?" Johnny had a fat face and no eyelashes, and wore a muffler instead of a collar. "I say, give me a wild one." The man with *The Morning Post* went on to talk about rabbits and the price at which he had sold them. At intervals, during everything he said, Johnny kept nodding and saying, with a smile of relish: "Give me a wild one!" He said it even when the talk had drifted altogether away from rabbits. He went on repeating it to himself in lower tones, as though at last he had found a thought that suited him. "Municipalisation means jobbery," said the young man with the bowler hat; "look at the County Council tramways." "Give me a wild one," said Johnny, in a dreamy whisper; "*I* say, give me a wild one." "Why, it stands to reason, if you have a friend, and you see a chance of shovin' him into a job at the public expense, you'll do it, won't you?" said the young man, addressing the reader of *The Morning Post*, who merely cleared his throat nervously in answer. "It's human nature," said the young man. "Give me a wild one," whispered Johnny. "I'm afraid there's going to be trouble in Ireland," the man with *The Morning Post* turned the subject. The young man was ready for him. "There will always be trouble in Ireland," he said, with what the novelists describe as a curl of his lip, "so long as Ireland exists." The tramp continued to mumble about the condition of his friend's nose, Johnny relapsed into silence, and the young man made the man with *The Morning Post* tremble by a horrible picture of what the country would be like under a Labour Government. "It would be all U.P.," he said firmly; "all up. . . ." Who would travel in such days if he could possibly avoid it?

XV

THE MOST CURIOUS ANIMAL

Curiosity is the first of the sins. On the day on which Eve gave way to her curiosity, man broke off his communion with the angels and allied himself with the beasts. To-day we usually applaud curiosity; we think of it as the alternative to stagnation. The tradition of mankind, however, is against us. The fables never pretend that curiosity is anything but an evil. Literature is full of tales of forbidden rooms that cannot be peeped into without disaster. Fatima in *Bluebeard* escapes punishment, but her escape is narrow enough to leave her a warning to the nursery. A version of the Pandora legend imputes the state of mankind to the curiosity of one disastrous fool who raised the lid of the sacred box, with the result that the blessings intended for our race escaped and flew away. We have cursed the inquisitive person through the centuries. We have instinctively hated him

to the point of persecution. The curious
among mankind have gone about their business
at peril of their lives. It is probable that
Athens was a city as much given to curiosity
as any city has ever been, and yet the Athen-
ians put Socrates to death on account of his
curiosity. He was accused of speculating
about the heavens above and inquiring into
the earth beneath as well as of corrupting the
youth and making the worse appear the better
reason. History may be read as the story of
the magnificent rearguard action fought during
several thousand years by dogma against
curiosity. Dogma is always in the majority
and is therefore detestable, but it is also always
beaten and is therefore admirable. It rallies
its forces afresh on some new field in every
generation. It fights with its back to the sun-
rise under a banner of darkness, but even
when we abominate it most we cannot but
marvel at its endurance. The odd thing is
that man clings to dogma from a sense of
safety. He can hardly help feeling that he
was never so safe as he is in the present in
possession of this little patch his fathers have
bequeathed to him. He felt quite safe without

printed books, without chloroform, without flying machines. He mocked at Icarus as the last word in human folly. We say nowadays " as safe as the Bank of England," but he felt safer without the Bank of England. We are told that when the Bank was founded in 1694 its institution was warmly opposed by all the dogmatic believers in things as they were. But it is against curiosity about knowledge that men have fought most stubbornly. Galileo was forbidden to be curious about the moon. One of the most difficult things to establish is our right to be curious about facts. The dogmatists offer to provide us with all the facts a reasonable man can desire. If we persist in believing that there is a world of facts yet undiscovered and that it is our duty to set out in quest of it, in the eyes of the dogmatists we are scorned as heretics and charlatans. Even at the present day, when the orthodoxies sit on shaky thrones, dogma still opposes itself to curiosity at many points. A great deal of the popular dislike of psychical research is due to hatred of curiosity in a new direction. People who admit the existence of a world of the dead commonly feel that none the less it ought to be taboo to the too-curious intellect of man. They feel there is something uncanny about spirits that makes it unsafe to approach them with an inquisitive mind. I am not concerned either to attack or defend Spiritualism. I merely suggest that a rational attack on Spiritualism must be based on the insufficiency of the evidence put forward in its behalf, not on the ground that the curiosity which goes in search of such evidence is in itself wicked.

It is odd to see how men who take sides with dogma give themselves the airs of men who live for duty, while they regard the more curious among their fellows as licentious, trifling, irreverent and self-indulgent. The truth is, there is no greater luxury than dogma. It puts an eminence under the most stupid. At the same time I am not going to deny the pleasures of curiosity. We have only to see a cat looking up the chimney or examining the nooks of a box-room or looking over the edge of a trunk to see what is inside in order to realise that this is a vice, if it is a vice, which we inherit from the animals. We find a comparable curiosity in children and other simple creatures. Servants will rummage through drawer after drawer of old, dull letters out of idle curiosity. There are men who declare that no woman could be trusted not to read a letter. We persuade ourselves that man is a higher animal, above curiosity and a slave to his sense of honour. But man, too, likes to spy upon his neighbours when he is not indifferent to them. No scrupulous person of either sex would read another person's letter surreptitiously. But that is not to say that we do not want to know what is in the letter. We can hardly see a parcel lying unopened in a hall without speculating on what it contains. We should always feel happier if the owner of the parcel indulged us to the point of opening it in our presence. I know a man whose curiosity extends so far as to set him uncorking any medicine-bottles he sees in a friend's house, sniffing at them, and even sipping them to see what they taste like. " Oh, I have had that one," he says, as he lingers over the bitter flavour of strychnine. " Let me see," he reflects, as he sips another bottle, " there's nux vomica in that." Half the interesting books of the world were written by men who had just this sipping kind of curiosity   Curiosity was the chief pleasure of Montaigne and of Boswell. We cannot read an early book of science without finding signs of the pleasure of curiosity in its pages. Theophrastus, we may be sure, was a happy man when he wrote:

"However, there is one question which applies to all perfumes, namely, why it is that they appear to be sweetest when they come from the wrist; so that perfumers apply the scent to this part."

To be curious about such matters would keep many a man entertained for an evening. Some people are so much in love with their curiosity that they object even to having it satisfied too quickly with an obvious explanation. We have an instance of this in a pleasant anecdote about Democritus, which Montaigne borrowed from Plutarch. Montaigne, who substitutes figs for cucumbers in the story, relates:

"Democritus, having eaten figs at his table that tasted of honey, fell presently to consider within himself whence they should derive this unusual sweetness; and to be satisfied in it, was about to rise from the table to see the place whence the figs had been gathered; which his maid observing, and having understood the cause, she smilingly told him that he need not trouble himself about that, for she had put them into a vessel in which there had been honey. He was vexed that she had thus deprived him of the occasion of this inquisition and robbed his curiosity of matter to work upon. 'Go thy way,' said he, 'thou hast done me wrong; but for all that I will seek out the cause, as if it were natural'; and would willingly have found out some true reason for a false and imaginary effect."

The novel-reader who becomes furious with someone for letting him into the secret of the end of the story is of the same mind as Democritus. "Go thy way," he says in effect, "thou hast done me wrong." The child protests in the same way to a too-informative elder: "You weren't to tell me!" He would like to wander in the garden paths of curiosity. He has no wish to be led off hurriedly into the schoolroom of knowledge. He instinctively loves to guess. He loves at least to guess at one moment and to be told the next.

PLEASURES OF IGNORANCE

The greater part of human curiosity has as little to be said for it—or against it—as a child's whim. It is an affair of the senses, and an extraordinarily innocent one. It is a vanity of the eye or ear. It is another form of the hatred of being left out. So many human beings do not like to miss things. We saw during Saturday's aeroplane raid how far men and women will go rather than miss things. Thousands of Londoners stood in the streets and at their windows and gazed at what seemed to be the approach of one of the plagues of Egypt. No plague of locusts ever came out of the sky with a greater air of the will to destruction. It was as though the eastern sky were hung with these monstrous insects, leisurely hovering over a people they meant to destroy. They had the cupidity of hawks at one moment. At another they had the innocence of a school of little fishes. Shell-smoke opened out among them like a sponge thrown into the water. It swelled into larger clouds monstrous in shape as the things doctors preserve in bottles. But the plague did not rest. One saw a little black aeroplane hurry across them, a mere water

156

THE MOST CURIOUS ANIMAL

beetle of a thing, and one wondered if a collision would send one of them to earth with broken wings. But one did not really know whether this was the manœuvre of an enemy or the daring of a friend. There was never a more astonishing spectacle. A desperate battle in the air would have been less of a surprise. But that there should have been nobody to interfere with them! . . . Yes, it was certainly a curious sight, and London was justified in putting its head out of its house, like a tortoise under its shell, till the bombs began to fall. Still, the more often they come the less curious we shall be about them. A few years ago we gladly paid five shillings for the pleasure of seeing an aeroplane float round a big field. There is a limit, however, to our curiosity even about German aeroplanes. Speaking for myself, I may say my curiosity is satisfied. I do not care if they never come again.

XVI

THE OLD INDIFFERENCE

IT was an old belief of the poets and the common people that nature was sympathetic towards human beings at certain great crises. Comets flared and the sun was darkened at the death of a great man. Even the death of a friend was supposed to bow nature with despair; and Milton in *Lycidas* mourned the friend he had lost in what nowadays seems to us the pasteboard hyperbole:

> The willows and the hazel copses green
> Shall now no more be seen
> Fanning their joyous leaves to thy soft lays.

It may be contended that Milton was here speaking, not of nature, but of his vision of nature; and certainly one cannot help reading one's own joys and sorrows into the face of the earth. When the lover in *Maud* affirms:

> A livelier emerald twinkled in the grass,

he states a fact. He utters a truth of the eye

and heart. The wonder of the world resides in him who sees it. The earth becomes a new place to a man who has fallen in love or who has just returned to it from the edge of the grave. It is as though he saw the flowers as a stranger. Larks ascending make the planet a ball of music for him. He may well begin to lie about nature, for he has seen it for the first time. Experience is not long in warning him, however, that it is he and not the world that has changed. He meets a funeral in the midsummer of his happiness, and larks sing the same songs above the fields whether it is the lover or the mourner that goes by. The continuity of nature is not broken either for our gladness or our grief. Mr Hardy frequently introduces the mournful drip of rain into his picture of men and women unhappily mated. But the rain is not at the beck and call of the unhappy. The unhappy would still be unhappy though they were in a cherry orchard on the loveliest morning of the year. The happy would still be happy though St Swithin's Day were streaming in floods down the window-panes. Who does not know what it is to be happy watching the rain-drops racing down the glass and hearing the gutter chattering

like a hedgeful of sparrows or tinkling like a
bell? Who is there, on the other hand, who
has not found, and been perplexed to find, the
world going on its way in full song and bloom
on a day that has seemed to him to darken all
human experience? Burns's reproach to the
indifferent earth has often been quoted as an
expression of this realisation that nature does
not mind:

> How can ye sing, ye little birds,
> And I sae weary, fu' o' care?

Nature, we discover, passes us and our sorrows
by. We are of little account to the race of birds.
We are of little account, for that matter, to the
race of men. The end of Hamlet is not the end
even of a kingdom. Fortinbras comes upon the
scene, and life goes on. Our mournings are only
interruptions. The ranks of the procession close
up and little is changed. Even the funeral of
a king is as a rule less an occasion for grief
than a spectacle for the curious. The crowd
may have filled the streets all night, but they
did not forget to bring their sandwiches and
whisky-flasks with them. The theatres and the
tea-shops and the public-houses will be as full

as ever the next day. And for the death of a great author not even the sweet-shops will be closed. The funeral ceremonies over the dead body of Herbert Spencer drew a smaller crowd than would gather to see a dog that had been run over in the street.

We were never before so conscious of the indifference of Nature to human tragedy as since the outbreak of the war. Here, one would think, was a tragedy that all but threatened to crack the globe. One would imagine that the sides of Nature must be in pain with it and the earth in peril of being hurled out of her accustomed path round the sun. Yet the sparrows in the Surrey valleys have not heard of it, and the sea-birds know nothing of it, save that occasionally they are bewildered to find a submarine rising from the waters instead of the porpoise for whose presence they had hoped. It is said that the pheasants in a Sussex wood awoke and screamed on Sunday night during the barrage fire around London. But this was egotism on the part of the pheasants. The pheasants of Wiltshire did not have their sleep broken, and so were not troubled about the sufferings of Londoners. Wordsworth assured Toussaint L'Ouverture:

PLEASURES OF IGNORANCE

> There's not a breathing of the common air
> That will forget thee.

He exaggerated. The common air is more perturbed in the year 1918 by the passing of a single gnat than by the memory of Toussaint L'Ouverture. On Sunday I walked along a quiet hill road within thirty miles of London, and it seemed for an hour or two as though one were as remote from the war as a man living a century hence. The catkins in the hazels by the roadside were beautiful as falling rain : they hung on the branches like notes of music. The country children see them as lambs' tails, dangling in twos and threes in the gentle air. They have been growing longer every day since Christmas, and the red tips of the female flowers have now begun to appear. In the hedge there are still the remains of old man's beard that, in one light, looks like dirty wool, but, with the sun shining on it, seems at a distance to be hawthorn in the full glory of blossom. Every now and then a crooked caterpillar of down is detached from it by the wind and sails off vaguely over a field. A few weeks ago sparrows were singing choruses as they gorged themselves upon it, but lately they have been scraping their beaks busily on the bark of trees as though they had found more satisfying dishes. At the lower end of the road there is a glow of crimson among the sallows, which have begun to festoon their straight rods with silver buds. Chaffinches are beginning to pipe more solitarily to each other in the tall elms. A few weeks ago they fluttered everywhere in companies, occupying now a hedge, now a road, and now a tree. The naturalists tell us that these winter companies of chaffinches are usually composed of birds of one sex only, the males consorting together for the time as in a boys' school. The chaffinch, I think, is the commonest bird in this part of the country. It is so common that its loveliness has hardly been appreciated as it ought to be. It is a little world of colour, like a small jay, and nothing could be more beautiful than its flushed breast as it sits on the top of a tall tree in the sunset. As for the jay, it hurries away like a thief before one has time to see its coat of many colours. The jay, like the cuckoo, is a bird with a guilty conscience. The wood here is full of jays, uttering their one monotonous shriek, like the ripping of a skirt. They scuttle among the trees at one's approach, showing the white feather. Occasionally, however, they too will sit in a tree and allow the sun to flush their cinnamon-coloured breasts. But we shall see hundreds of them before we see a single one in the crested and passive splendour of the jays in the picture-books. As a matter of fact, nearly all the birds in the picture-books are guesses and exaggerations. The birds, we discover before long, are a secret kingdom into which it is given to few to enter.

The whole of Nature, indeed, is curiously secretive. She does not tell much about herself save to the importunate. Not many of us can speak her language or have learned the password to her cave of treasure. She thrusts upon our notice a few birds, a few insects, a few animals, a few flowers. But for the most part there is no finding her population without seeking for it. Hundreds of her flowers are hidden from the lazy eye, and we may pass a lifetime without seeing so common a bird as a tree-creeper or so common an animal as a shrew-mouse. How seldom it is one sees even a rat! There are human beings who will never discover an early flower, however many miles they cover in their country walks. They take no pleasure in finding a wild-strawberry flower in January

or a campion blossom in the first week in
February. They are as indifferent to Nature
as Nature is to them. The honeysuckle that
breaks out with leaves as with green flames ;
the thrust of the leaves of the wild hyacinth
under the trees, like the return of youth ; the
flowering of the elm ; the young moon like a
white bird with spread wings in the afternoon
sky ; the golden journey of Orion and his dog
across the heavens by night—these things, they
feel, are not interwoven with man's fate. They
were before him, and they will be after him.
Therefore, he cares more for his little brick
house in the suburbs, which will at least be
changed when he goes. I do not suggest that
anyone consciously adopts a philosophy of this
kind. But most of us are undoubtedly a little
offended at some time in our lives when we
realise that Nature has so little regard for our
passions and our tears. She is a consoler, but
it is on her own terms. Matthew Arnold found
the secret of life in becoming as resigned to
obedience as the stars and the tide. Who knows
but, if we do this, Nature may be found to care
after all ? But she does not care in the way in
which most of us want her to care. The religious

discovered that long ago. They found that Nature was guilty of neutrality in human affairs, if they did not go further and suspect her of enmity. It is only when philosophy has been added to religion that men have been able to reconcile without gloom the indifference of Nature with the idea of the love of God. And even the religious and the philosophers are puzzled by the spectacle of the worm that writhes on the garden path while the robin pecks at it, triumphant in his fatness and praising the fine weather.

XVII

EGGS: AN EASTER HOMILY

HAVING decided to write on Easter, I took out
a volume of *The Encyclopædia Britannica* in order
to make up the subject of eggs, and the first
entry under "Egg" that met my eye was:

"EGG, AUGUSTUS LEOPOLD (1816–1863),
English painter, was born on the 2nd of May,
1816, in London, where his father carried on
business as a gun-maker."

I wish I had known about Augustus five
years ago. I should like to have celebrated
the centenary of an egg somewhere else than
in a London tea-shop. Augustus Leopold Egg
seems to have spent a life in keeping with his
name. He was taught drawing by Mr Sass,
and in later years was a devotee of amateur
theatricals, making a memorable appearance,
as we should expect of an Egg, in a play called
Not so Bad as We Seem. He also appears to
have devoted a great part of his life to painting
bad eggs, if we may judge by the titles of

his most famous pictures — *Buckingham Rebuffed, Queen Elizabeth discovers she is no longer young, Peter the Great sees Catherine for the First Time,* and *Past and Present, a Triple Picture of a Faithless Wife.* She was a lady, no doubt, who could not submit to the marriage yolk. Anyhow, she had a great fall, and Augustus did his best to put her together again. " Egg," the *Encyclopædia* tells us finally, " was rather below the middle height, with dark hair and a handsome, well-formed face." He seems to have been a man, take him for all in all : we shall not look upon his like again.

Even so, Augustus was not the only Egg. He was certainly not the egg in search of which I opened the *Encyclopædia.* The egg I was looking for was the Easter egg, and it seemed to be the only egg that was not mentioned. There were birds' eggs, and reptiles' eggs, and fishes' eggs, and molluscs' eggs, and crustaceans' eggs, and insects' eggs, and frogs' eggs, and Augustus Egg, and the eggs of the duck-billed platypus, which is the only mammal (except the spiny ant-eater) whose eggs are " provided with a large store of yolk, enclosed within a shell, and extruded to undergo development apart from the maternal tissues." I do not know whether it is evidence of the irrelevance of the workings of the human mind or of our implacable greed of knowledge, but within five minutes I was deep in the subject of eggs in general, and had forgotten all about the Easter variety. I found myself fascinated especially by the eggs of fishes. There are so many of them that one was impressed as one is on being told the population of London. " It has been calculated," says the writer of the article, " that the number laid by the salmon is roughly about 1000 to every pound weight of the fish, a 15-lb. salmon laying 15,000 eggs. The sturgeon lays about 7,000,000; the herring 50,000; the turbot 14,311,000; the sole 134,000; the perch 280,000." This is the sort of sentence I always read over to myself several times. And when I come to " the turbot, 14,311,000," I pause, and try to picture to myself the man who counted them. How does one count 14,311,000 ? How long does it take? If one lay awake all night, trying to put oneself to sleep by counting turbots' eggs instead of sheep, one would hardly have done more than make a fair start by the time the maid came in to draw the curtains and let in the sun on one's exhausted temples. A person like myself, ignorant of mathematics, could not easily count more that 10,000 in an hour. This would mean that, even if one lay in bed for ten hours, which one never does except on one's birthday, one would have counted only 100,000 out of the 14,311,000 eggs by the time one had to get up for breakfast. That would leave 14,211,000 still to be counted. At this point, most of us, I think, would give it up in despair. After one horrible night's experience, we would jump into a hot bath, muttering: "Never again! Never again!" like a statesman who can't think of anything to say, and send out for a quinine-and-iron tonic. Our friends meeting us later in the day would say with concern: "Hullo! you're looking rather cheap. What have you been doing?"; and when we answered bitterly: "Counting turbots' eggs," they would hurry off with an apprehensive look on their faces. The naturalist, it is clear, must be capable of a persistence that is beyond the reach of most of us. I calculate that, if he were able to work for 14 hours a

day, counting at the rate of 10,000 an hour,
even then it would take him 122·214 days to
count the eggs of a single turbot.   After that,
it would take a chartered accountant at least
122·214 days to check his figures.   One can
gather from this some idea of the enormous
industry of men of science.   For myself, I
could more easily paint the Sistine Madonna
or compose a Tenth Symphony than be content
to loose myself into this universe of numbers.
Pythagoras, I believe, discovered a sort of
philosophy in numbers, but even he did not
count beyond seven.

After the fishes, the reptiles seem fairly
modest creatures.   The ordinary snake does
not lay more than twenty or thirty eggs, and
even the python is content to stop at a hundred.
The crocodile, though a wicked animal, lays
only twenty or thirty; the tortoise as few
as two or four; and the turtle does not
exceed two hundred.   But I am not really·
interested in eggs—not, at least, in any eggs
but birds' eggs—or should not have been, if I
had not read *The Encyclopædia Britannica*.   The
sight of a fly's egg—if the fly lays an egg—fills
me with disgust—and frogs' eggs attract me

only with the fascination of repulsion. What one likes about the birds is that they lay such pretty eggs. Even the duck lays a pretty egg. The duck is a plain bird, rather like a char-woman, but it lays an egg which is (or can be) as lovely as an opal. The flavour, I agree, is not Christian, but, like other eggs of which this can be said, it does for cooking. Hens' eggs are less attractive in colour, but more varied. I have always thought it one of the chief miseries of being a man that, when boiled eggs are put on the table, one does not get first choice, and that all the little brown eggs are taken by women and children before one's own turn comes round. There is one sort of egg with a beautiful sunburnt look that always reminds me of the seaside, and that I have not tasted in a private house for above twenty years. To begin the day with such an egg would put one in a good temper for a couple of hours. But always one is fobbed off with a large white egg of demonstrative un-comeliness. It may taste all right, but it does not look all right. Food should appeal to the eye as well as to the palate, as everyone recognises when the blancmange that has not set is brought to the table. At the same time, there is one sort of white egg that is quite delightful to look at. I do not know its parent, but I think it is a black hen of the breed called Spanish. Not everything white in Nature is beautiful. One dislikes instinctively white calves, white horses, white elephants and white waistcoats. But the particular egg of which I speak is one of the beautiful white things—like snow, or a breaking wave, or teeth. So certain am I, however, that neither it nor the little brown one will ever come my way, while there is a woman or a child or a guest to prevent it, that when I am asked how I like the eggs to be done I make it a point to say " poached " or " fried." It gives me at least a chance of getting one of the sort of eggs I like by accident. As for poached eggs, I agree. There are nine ways of poaching eggs, and each of them is worse than the other. Still, there is one good thing about poached eggs : one is never disappointed. One accepts a poached egg like fate. There is no sitting on tenterhooks, watching and waiting and wondering, as there is in regard to boiled eggs. I admit that most of the difficulties associated with boiled eggs could be got over by the use of egg-cosies — appurtenances of the breakfast-table that stirred me to the very depths of delight when I first set eyes on them as a child. It was at a mothers' meeting, where I was the only male present. Thousands of women sat round me, sewing and knitting things for a church bazaar. Much might be written about egg-cosies. Much might be said for and much against. They would be effective, however, only if it were regarded as a point of honour not to look under the cosy before choosing the egg. And the sense of honour, they say, is a purely masculine attribute. Children never had it, and women have lost it. I do not know a single woman whom I would trust not to look under an egg-cosy—not, at least, unless she were forbidden eggs by the doctor. In that case, any egg would seem delicious, and she would seize the nearest, irrespective of class or colour.

This may not explain the connection between eggs and Easter. But then neither does *The Encyclopædia Britannica.* I have looked up both the article on eggs and the article on Easter, and in neither of them can I find anything more relevant than such remarks as that

EGGS : AN EASTER HOMILY

" the eggs of the lizard are always white or yellowish, and generally soft-shelled; but the geckos and the green lizards lay hard-shelled eggs," or " Gregory of Tours relates that in 577 there was a doubt about Easter." In order to learn something about Easter eggs one has to turn to some such work as *The Dictionary of Phrase and Fable,* which tells us that " the practice of presenting eggs to our friends at Easter is Magian or Persian, and bears allusion to the mundane egg, for which Ormuzd and Ahriman were to contend till the consummation of all things." The advantage of reading *Tit-Bits* is that one gets to know hundreds of things like that. The advantage of not reading *Tit-Bits* is that one is so ignorant of them that a piece of information of this sort is as fresh and unexpected as the morning's news every Easter Monday. Next Easter, I feel sure, I shall look it up again. I shall have forgotten all about the mundane egg, even if Ormuzd and Ahriman have not. I shall be thinking more about my breakfast egg. What a piece of work is a man ! And yet many profound things might be said about eggs, mundane or otherwise. I wish I could have thought of them.

XVIII

ENTER THE SPRING

ONE would imagine from the way in which some people are talking that this is an early spring. I do not think it is. The daffodils certainly came before the swallows dared, but they came reluctantly and in less generous profusion than usual—at least, in one county. As for the swallow, it may have arrived by Saturday, but it has not arrived on the day on which I am writing. "About the middle of March," says Mr Coward, "the first swallows arrive," but I have met no one who has seen one even in the first week in April. The sky seems empty without them. This is, no doubt, an illusion. There are plenty of rooks and pigeons, and there are always starlings desperately hustling from the chimney-pot across to the plum-tree and back again. But the starling is most interesting, not when he is in the air, but when he is at rest—making queer noises in his effulgent, tight-fitting clothes, some-

times like a baby in a cradle, sometimes like
a girl trying to whistle, always experimenting
with sound rather than singing. One looks
forward to the swallows and martins and swifts
because they really do live the life of the air.
The sky is their domain, and no roof or tree or
even telegraph wire. Till they arrive the air
is an all but stagnant pool. They transform
it into a scene of whirlpools. They do for the
air what the hum of insects does for the garden.
They banish the stillness of winter and lead the
year in the movements of a remembered dance.

Spring, however, awakens gradually, and
does not plunge precipitately into an orgy.
First, the home birds sing, or rather redouble
their singing, for the wren and the robin
hardly ever left off. This, I think, must be an
exceptional year for the chorus of wrens. Last
year the lane that leads to the station was at
this time a lane of chaffinches: this year it is
a lane of wrens. Last year the garden was a
garden of thrushes: this year it is a garden of
wrens. That is possibly an exaggeration, but
this little Tetrazzini among the birds has
never seemed to me to trill so dominantly and
over so wide a rule. As for the thrushes, I do

not know what has happened to them. I
heard plenty of them on the outskirts of
London in February, but here, fifty miles from
London, it is as though they were an exterminated race. Whether gardeners or cats or
some other epidemic is to blame, the trees are
silent of them. Even the blackbird is not too
common here this year, but then a country
gardener regards a blackbird as a Turk regards
an Armenian. I wish thrushes and blackbirds
could read, so that one could put up a notice
offering them sanctuary even at the expense of
one's gooseberries and strawberries. Strange
that a strawberry should appear more delightful to anyone than the song of a blackbird! I
know, I may say, the feeling of helpless rage
that wells up in the human breast at the sight
of a blackbird stealing one's strawberries.
Thank God, I am not impervious to moral
indignation. If shouting "Stop thief!" could
save the strawberries, my voice would be for
saving them. But I do not believe in capital
punishment for petty theft, and, anyhow, if I
must lose either a song or a strawberry, I had
rather lose the strawberry.

The larks luckily take to the fields and

do not trust themselves near either cats or gardeners. They do not always escape even in the fields, and the dead bodies of some of them are served in a pudding in a Fleet Street restaurant. But, on the whole, considering what a dangerous neighbour man is, they escape fairly lightly. There is a sort of "live and let live" truce between them and the human race. The chaffinches, too—the greatest bird multitude there is, perhaps, after the house-sparrows—are free enough to sing. They have been, during the past week, sailing out on short voyages from the tops of trees, like fly-catchers, dancing in the air after their victims and then returning to the spray. The green-finch—that beautiful-winged Mrs Gummidge among birds—is also abundant, and slips down nervously every now and then among the groundsel in the unweeded garden. I confess the greenfinch has all my sympathy, but it rather bores me. What the deuce is it worry-ing about? There is no poetry in its lamenta-tion—only a sort of habitual formula of a poor, lorn woman. If birds could read, I think I should add to the notices I put up a little board containing the words :

PLEASURES OF IGNORANCE

> " No bottles,
> No hawkers,
> No greenfinches."

I should feel really sorry if they took any notice of my notice, but it might convey a hint to them that it would be good policy on their part to cheer up for at least five minutes in the day and that, in any case, there is no need to say the same thing over and over again. Every bird, it is true, says the same thing over and over again—at any rate, more or less the same thing. Birds such as the robin and the thrush vary their song as the chaffinch and the willow-wren do not. But even the robin and the thrush have a recognisable pattern. Fortunately, they are not always, like the greenfinch, thinking of the old 'un and thinking out loud.

The goldfinches have begun to fly about the garden again with their little sequins of song, as someone has delightfully described their music. They have their eyes, I hope, on the pear-tree—now as white as an Alp—where they built and brought up a large family last year. The cornflowers in the flower border are already in bud, and I am told that this is the temptation to which goldfinches most

easily yield. I hope so, at any rate. I should
have a garden blue with cornflowers, if I were
sure that this would entice the seven colours
of the goldfinch to make their home in it.
Last Saturday, two lesser spotted woodpeckers
invaded the garden. One always imagines a
woodpecker as a bird of more substantial size,
and it is surprising to see this little creature,
patterned on the back like something made in
the Omega workshop, no bigger than a sparrow,
as it hastily visits apple and fig tree and even
wygelia. As it climbed the wygelia, indeed,
a sparrow stooped down from an upper branch
to study it, and then advanced in the direction
of the woodpecker. The woodpecker lay back
from the trunk of the tree—lying on its back
in the air, as it were, and fluttering its wings
while holding on with its claws—and seemed
to invite the sparrow to come on. I don't
think the sparrow had ever seen a woodpecker
before. Its curiosity rather than its wrath
was aroused by the strange spectacle. It did
not want to hurt the foreigner, but only to
look at him. After having looked its fill, it
moved off to a safer tree. Then the woodpecker, whose heart had no doubt been in its

boots for the past five minutes, also loosed its
hold on the bark and made off over the gate
for a less exciting garden.

Outside the garden the spring began on
Good Friday. It came in with the chiffchaff.
For three years in succession I have heard the
first chiffchaff in exactly the same place—a
clump of nut-trees on the top of a high bank.
At this time of year, too, before the leaves are
out, it is easy to see it. And there are few
more charming birds to watch. With its little
beak as slender as a grass-seed, and its body
moving among the branches like a tiny shadow
rather than flesh and bones, it pauses again
and again in the midst of its eating to take an
upward glance and utter its mite of music—
as monotonous as a Thibetan's praying wheel.
Still lovelier is the willow-wren that follows it.
It is as though the chiffchaff were the first
sketch of a willow-wren. The willow-wren is
the perfected work of art, with little shades of
green added and a voice that, small though its
range is, is perhaps the most exquisite that
will fill the air till the nightingale arrives.
When I went out on Sunday morning, I prophesied that I would hear the first willow-wren,

and, though I heard only one in a hill-side
copse where the cowslips are just getting their
bells ready, the prophecy came true. Not
that I am much of a prophet. I don't know
how often I have prophesied the arrival of the
swallow. And, indeed, it is the surprises in
nature, rather than the things that one fore-
sees, that are the pleasantest—especially if one
is easily surprised, as I am. Whoever ceases
to be surprised, for instance, by the sight of a
goldcrested wren? I heard its tiny pinpoint
of voice last Sunday afternoon when I was
walking past a plantation where the bullace
was in flower, and, on looking into the trees,
saw the little thimble-sized creature making
free with invisible insects—his beak is hardly
big enough to eat a visible one—and performing acrobatics like a tit. One of the charms
of the goldcrest is that he does not look on a
human being as a wild beast. The blackbird
regards a man as a policeman; the greenfinch
bolts for it if you so much as look at him, but
the goldcrest feels as secure in your presence
as if you were behind bars in a cage in the
Zoological Gardens. One could probably make
him jump if one went up to him and shouted

suddenly into his ear, or even by making a violent gesture. But his first instinct is not to run. That, for a bird, is a considerable compliment. There can be nothing more distressing to a man of strictly honourable intentions than to have to creep about hedges furtively like a criminal in order to get a good look at a bird. Why he should want to look at birds at all it is difficult to explain. I suppose it is a sort of disease, like going to the "movies" or doing exercises. All I know is that, if you get it, you get it very badly. You would stop Shakespeare himself, if he were reciting a new sonnet to you, and bid him be quiet and look half-way up the elm where the nuthatch was beating away—up and down, like a blacksmith —at a nut or something in a knob of the tree. St Paul might be reading out to you the first draft of his Epistle to the Romans; you would quite unscrupulously interrupt him with a "Hush, man! There's a tree-creeper somewhere about. Listen, there he is! If you keep quiet, perhaps we'll be able to see him." I assure you, it is as bad as that. As for a man who takes out a noisy dog, or who whacks at loose stones with his stick on the road, you would regard him as a misbehaved and riotous person and would not call him your friend. Everything has to be subordinated to the hope of catching sight of a hypothetical bird—which you have probably seen dozens of times already. Truly, there is no accounting for human vices. There is, however, at least this to be said in favour of bird-watching, that it is the pleasantest of the vices, that it is cheaper than golf, and does not harden the arteries like tea-drinking. And after all, if one is going to get excited at all, one may as well get excited about the colours and songs of birds as about most things.

XIX

THE DAREDEVIL BARBER

To roll over Niagara Falls in a barrel is an odd
way of courting death, but it seems that death
must be courted somehow. Danger is more
attractive to many men than drink. They prefer gambling with their lives to gambling with
their money. They have the gambler's faith
in their lucky star. They are preoccupied with
the vision of victory to the exclusion of all timid
thoughts. They have a dramatic sense that sets
them anticipatorily on a stage, bowing to the
applause of the multitude. It is the applause,
I fancy, rather than the peril itself, that entices
them. The average boy who performs a deed
of derring-do performs it before his admiring
fellows. Even in so small a thing as ringing a
bell and running away he likes to have spec-
tators. Few boys ring bells out of mischief when
they are alone. Poor Mr Charles Stephens, the
" Daredevil Barber " of Bristol, who lost his life

THE DAREDEVIL BARBER

at Niagara Falls in his six-foot barrel the other Sunday, made sure that there would be plenty of witnesses of his adventure. Not only had he a party of sightseers in motors along the road following the cask on its perilous voyage but he had a cinematograph photographer ready to immortalise the affair on a film. Two other persons, it is said, had already accomplished a similar feat. One of them, a woman, "was just about gone," according to a witness, "when we got her out of the barrel." The other "was a used-up man for several weeks." This however, did not deter the daredevil barber. Had he not already on one occasion put his head into a lion's mouth? Had he not boxed in a lion's den? Had he not stood up to men with rifles who shot lumps of sugar from his head? It may seem an extraordinary way to behave in a world in which there are so many reasonable opportunities for heroism, but men are extraordinary creatures. There is no adventure so wild that they will not embark on it. There are men who, if they took it into their heads that there was one chance in a hundred of reaching the moon by being precipitated into space in some kind of torpedo, would volunteer for the adventure. They do these mad things alike for trivial and noble ends. They love a stunt even (or especially) at the risk of their lives. Half the aeroplane accidents are due to the fact that many men prefer risk to safety. To do some things that other people cannot do seems to them the only way of justifying their existence. It is an initiation into aristocracy. Every man is the rival of all other men, and he is not satisfied till he has beaten them. If he is a great cricketer, or a great poet, or a Cabinet Minister, or wins the Derby, his ambition as a rule is fulfilled and he does not feel the need of jumping down Etna or hanging by his toes from the Eiffel Tower in order to create a sensation. But if a man is no use at either poetry or football, he must do something. Blondin became a world-famous figure simply by walking along a tight-rope along which neither Shakespeare nor Shelley could have walked. It may be that they would have had no desire to walk along it, but in any case Blondin was able to feel that he could beat the greatest of men in at least one game. In his own business he stood above the Apostle Paul and Michelangelo and Napoleon. He was a king and, even if you

THE DAREDEVIL BARBER

did not envy him his trade, you had to envy him his throne. He was a man you would have liked to meet at dinner, not for the sake of his conversation, but for the sake of his uniqueness. One remembers how one stood with heart in mouth as he set out with his balancing-pole in his hand on his journey across the rope blindfolded and pretending to stumble every ten yards. A single false step and he would have fallen from the height of a tower to certain death, for there was no net to catch him. Strange that one should have cared whether he fell or not! But ninety-nine out of a hundred did care. We watched him as breathlessly as though he were carrying the future of the world in his hands. He knew that he was interesting us, engrossing us, and that was his reward. It was a reward, no doubt, that could be measured in gold. But it is more than greed of gold that sets men courting death in such ways. The joy of being unique is at least as great as the joy of being rich. And the surest way of becoming unique is to trail one's coat in the presence of Death and challenge him to tread on the tail of it.

Not that even the most daring seeker after

uniqueness fails to take numerous precautions for his safety. No man is mad enough to set out along a tight-rope in hobnailed boots without previous practice. No woman who has not learned to swim has ever tried to swim the English Channel from Dover to Cape Grisnez. Even the daredevil barber of Bristol insured himself, so far as he could, against the perils of his adventure. He had an oxygen tank in the barrel which would have kept him alive for a time if the barrel had not been swept under the Falls, and he had friends patrolling the waters to recover the barrel. Like the schoolboy who takes risks, he did not feel that he was going to get caught. "I have the greatest confidence," he said, "that I shall come through all right." His previous escapes must have given him the assurance that he was not born to die of danger. Not only had he served through the war, but he had once plucked a woman from the railway line when the express was so near that it tore her skirt. He must have felt that one man at least could live in perfect safety in the kingdom of danger. He was probably less nervous as he crept into his barrel than a schoolgirl would be in getting into the boat on the chute. He had' we may be sure, his thrill, but was it the thrill of being in peril or the thrill of being conspicuous? Some men, of course, there are who love danger for danger's sake, and who would run risks in an empty world. Men of this kind make good spies, and, in their youth, good burglars. Theirs is the desire of the moth for the star—or at any rate of the moth that feels it is different from every other moth and can successfully dare the candle flame. To play with fire and not to be consumed is a universal pleasure. The child passes its finger through the gas-flame and glories in the sensation. It is like playing a game of touch with danger. The triumph of escape gives one a delicious moment. That is why many men invent dangers for themselves. It is simply for the pleasure of escaping them. There are boys who enjoy wrenching knockers off doors, not because knockers are an interesting kind of bric-à-brac, but because there is just a chance of being caught in the act by the police. I once knew a youth who had a drawer filled with knockers. He felt as proud of them as a young Indian would have been of an equal number of the scalps of his enemies. They proved that he was a brave. Every man would like to be a brave, though every man dare not. I confess I never had much ambition to wrench knockers, but that may have been because I was perfectly content with the world as it is without making it any more dangerous. I often think that people who put their heads into lions' mouths do not realise what a dangerous place the planet is without any artificial stimulus.

Did the daredevil barber of Bristol ever realise, I wonder, the danger he was in every time he raised a fork with a piece of roast beef to his lips ? Either the beef might have choked him or it might have given him ptomaine poisoning, or, if it failed of either of these, there are at least half-a-dozen fatal diseases which vegetarians say are caused by eating it. Even if we take for granted that there is little danger in plain beef, are there not curries and sausages and pork-pies on which a lover of risks may exercise his daring in the restaurants ? I know people who are afraid to eat fish on a Monday lest it may have gone bad over the week-end. Others live in terror of mackerel and herrings. I myself have always admired the gallantry of Londoners who go into a chance restaurant and order lobster or curried prawns. Then there are all the tinned foods, a spoil for heroes. I have known a V.C. who was frightened of tinned salmon. And a man's food is not more beset with perils than his drink. Even if he confines himself to water, he is in danger at every sip. If the water is too hard, it may deposit destruction in his arteries. If it is too soft, it may give his child rickets. Or it may be populous with germs and give him typhoid fever. If, on the other hand, he is dissatisfied with the drink of the beasts and takes to beverages the use of which distinguishes men from oxen, what a nightmare procession of potential ills lies in wait for him! You may read an account of them in any temperance tract. The very enumeration of them would drive a weak man to water, if water itself were not suspect. But, alas, even to breathe is to put oneself in danger. There are more germs in a bus than there are stars in the firmament, and one cannot walk along the Strand without all sorts of bacilli shooting their little arrows at one at every breath. If men realised these things — truly realised them— they would see that there is no need to go to the North Pole in order to live dangerously. A walk from Charing Cross to St Paul's would then be seen to be as rich in hairbreadth escapes as a voyage to an island of head-hunters. The man who lives the most thrilling life I know is a man who rarely stirs beyond his garden. Every time he is pricked by a thorn or gets a little earth in his finger-nail, he rushes into the house to bathe his hands in lysol and, for days afterwards, he keeps feeling his jaw to see whether it is stiffening with the first signs of tetanus. He lives in a condition of recurrent alarm. He gets more frights in a week than an ordinary traveller could get in a year. I have often advised him to give up gardening, seeing that he finds it so exciting. I have come to the conclusion, however, that he enjoys those half-hourly rushes to the lysol-bottle—the desperate game of hide-and-seek with lockjaw. He needs no barrel to roll him over Niagara in order to gaze into "the bright eyes of danger." He finds all the danger he wants at the root of the meanest brussels sprout that blows.

XX

WEEDS: AN APPRECIATION

A WEED, says the dictionary, is "any plant that is useless, troublesome, noxious or grows where it is not wanted." The dictionary also adds: "*colloq.*, a cigar." We may omit for our present purpose the harmless colloquialism, but the rest of the definition deserves to be closely examined. Socrates, I imagine, could have found a number of pointed questions to put to the dictionary maker. He might have begun with two of the commonest weeds, the nettle and the dandelion. Having got his opponent—and the opponents of Socrates were all of the same mental build as Sherlock Holmes's Dr Watson—eagerly to admit that the nettle was a weed, he would at once put the definition to the test. "The story goes," he would say, quoting Mrs Clark Nuttall's admirable work, *Wild Flowers as They Grow*, "that the Roman soldiers brought the most venomous of the stinging nettles to England to flagellate themselves with when they were benumbed with the cold of this—to them— terribly inclement isle. It is certain," he would add from the same source, "that physicians at one time employed nettles to sting paralysed limbs into vigour again, also to cure rheumatism. In view of all this," he would ask, "does it not follow either that the nettle is not a weed or that your definition of a weed is mistaken?" And his opponent would be certain to answer: "It does follow, O Socrates." A second opponent, however, would rashly take up the argument. He would point out that even if the Romans had a mistaken notion that nettle-stings were useful as a preventive of cold feet, and if our superstitious ancestors made use of them to cure rheumatism, as our superstitious contemporaries resort to bee-stings for the same purpose, the nettle was at all times probably useless and is certainly useless to-day. Socrates would turn to him with a quiet smile and ask: "When we say that a plant is useless, do we mean merely that we as a matter of fact make no use of it, or that it would be of no use even if we did make use of it?" And the reply would leap out: "Undoubtedly the latter, O Socrates." Socrates would then remember his Mrs Nuttall again, and refer to an old herbal which claimed that "excessive corpulency may be reduced" by taking a few nettle-seeds daily. He would admit that he had never made a trial of this cure, as he had no desire to get rid of the corpulency with which the gods had seen fit to endow him. He would claim, however, that the usefulness of the nettle had been proved as an article of diet, that it was once a favourite vegetable in Scotland, that it had helped to keep people alive at the time of the Irish famine, and that even during the recent war it had been recommended as an excellent substitute for spinach. "May we not put it in this way," he would ask, "that you call a nettle useless merely because you yourself do not make use of it?" "It seems that you are right, O Socrates." "And would you call an aeroplane useless, merely because you yourself have never made use of an aeroplane? Or a pig useless, merely because you yourself do not eat pork?" There would be a great wagging of heads among the opponents, after which a third would pluck up courage to say : " But, surely, Socrates, nettles as we know them to-day are simply noxious plants that fulfil no function but to sting our children?" Socrates would say, after a moment's pause : "That certainly is an argument that deserves serious consideration. A weed, then, is to be condemned, you think, not for its uselessness, but for its noxiousness?" This would be agreed to. "Then," he would pursue his questions, "you would probably call monkshood a weed, seeing that it has been the cause not merely of pain but even of death itself to many children." His opponent would grow angry at this, and exclaim : "Why, I cultivate monkshood in my own garden. It is one of the most beautiful of the flowers." Then there would be some wrangling as to whether ugliness was the test of weeds, till Socrates would make it clear that this would involve omitting speedwell and the scarlet pimpernel from the list. Someone else would contend that the essence of a weed was its troublesomeness, but Socrates would counter this by asking them whether horseradish was not a far more troublesome thing in a garden than foxgloves. "Oh," one of the disputants

WEEDS : AN APPRECIATION

would cry in desperation, "let us simply say
that a weed is any plant that is not wanted in
the place where it is growing." "You would
call groundsel a weed in the garden of a man
who does not keep a canary, but not a weed in
the garden of a man who does?" "I would."
Socrates would burst out laughing at this, and
say : "It seems to me that a weed is more
difficult to define even than justice. I think
we had better change the subject and talk
about the immortality of the soul." The only
part of the definition of a weed, indeed, that
bears a moment's investigation is contained in
the three words : "*colloq.*, a cigar."

In my opinion, the safest course is to in-
clude among weeds all plants that grow wild.
It is also important to get rid of the notion that
weeds are necessarily evil things that should be
exterminated like rats. I remember some years
ago seeing an appalling suggestion that farmers
should be compelled by law to clear their land
of weeds. The writer, if I remember correctly,
even looked forward to the day when a farmer
would be fined if a daisy were found growing in
one of his fields. Utilitarianism of this kind
terrifies the imagination. There are some

people who are aghast at the prospect of a world of simplified spelling. But a world of simplified spelling would be Arcadia itself compared to a world without wild flowers. According to certain writers in *The Times*, however, we are faced with the possibility of a world without wild flowers, even if the Board of Agriculture takes no hand in the business. These writers tell us that the reckless plucking of wild flowers has already led to a great diminution in their numbers. Daffodils grow wild in many parts of England, but, as soon as they appear, hordes of holiday-makers rush to the scene and gather them in such numbers as to injure the life of the plants. I am not enough of a botanist to know whether it is possible in this way to discourage flowers that grow from bulbs. If it is, it seems likely enough that, with the increasing popularity of country walks, there will after a time be no daffodils or orchises left in England. If one were sure of it, one would never pluck a bee-orchis again. One does not know why one plucks it, except that the bee-shaped flower is one of the most exquisite of Nature's toys, and one is greedy of possessing it. Children try to

catch butterflies for the same reason. If it
were possible to catch a sunset or a blue sea,
no doubt we should take them home with us,
too. It may be that art is only the transmuted
instinct to seize and make our own all the
beautiful things we see. The collector of birds'
eggs and the painter are both collectors of a
beauty that can be known only in hints and
fragments. Still, the painter is justified by the
fact that his borrowings actually add to the
number of beautiful things. If the collector
of eggs and the gatherer of flowers can be shown
to be actually anti-social in their greed, we
cannot be so enthusiastic about them. I confess
that on these matters I have an open mind.
For all I know, the discussion on wild flowers
in *The Times* may be merely a scare. At the
same time, it seems reasonable to believe that
if flowers that propagate themselves from seed
were all gathered as soon as they appeared, there
would before long be no flowers left. I notice
that one suggestion has been made to the effect
that flower-lovers should provide themselves
with seeds and should scatter these in "likely
places" during their country walks. I do not
like this plotting on Nature's behalf. Besides,

it might lead to some rather difficult situations. If this general seed-sowing became a matter of principle, for instance, I should probably sow daisies on my neighbour's tennis lawn, poppies and fumitory in his cornfield, and dandelions in his meadow. It is not that I am devoted to the dandelion as a flower, though it has been praised for its beauty, but at a later stage a meadow of a million dandelion-clocks seems to me to be one of the most beautiful of spectacles. But I would go further than this. I should never see a hill-side cultivated without going out at night and sowing it with the seeds of gorse and thistle. Not that I should bear any ill-will to the farmer, but it is said that the diminution of waste land, with its abundance of gorse and thistles, has led to a great diminution in the number of linnets and goldfinches. The farmer, perhaps, can do without linnets and goldfinches, but we who make our living in other ways cannot. I should sow tares among his wheat, if necessary, if I believed that tares would tempt a bearded tit or a golden oriole.

Still, I cannot easily persuade myself that a Society for the Protection of Weeds is even now necessary. I have great faith in weeds.

WEEDS : AN APPRECIATION

If they are given a fair chance, I should back
them against any cultivated flower or vegetable
I know. Anyone who has ever had a garden
knows that, while it is necessary to work hard
to keep the shepherd's purse and the chickweed and the dandelion and the wartwort and
the hawkweed and the valerian from growing,
one has to take no such pains in order to keep
the lettuces and the potatoes from growing.
For myself, I should, in the vulgar phrase,
back the shepherd's purse against the lettuces
every time. If the weeds in the garden fail to
make us radiantly happy, it is not because they
are weeds, but because they are the wrong
weeds. Why not the ground-ivy instead of
the shepherd's purse, that lank intruder that
not only is a weed but looks like one ? Why
not bee-orchises for wartwort, and gentians for
chickweed ? I have no fault to find with the
foxgloves under the apple-tree or with the ivy-
leaved toad-flax that hangs with its elfin flowers
from every cranny in the wall. But I protest
against the dandelions and the superfluity of
groundsel. I undertake that, if rest-harrow
and scabious and corn-cockle invade the garden,
I shall never use a hoe on them. More than

this, if only the right weeds settled in the garden, I should grow no other flowers. But shepherd's purse! Compared with it, a cabbage is a posy for a bridesmaid, and sprouting broccoli a bouquet for a prima donna. After all, one ought to be allowed to choose the weeds for one's own garden. But then, when one chooses them, one no longer calls them weeds. The periwinkle, the primrose and the mallow — we spare them with our tongue as with our hoe. This, perhaps, suggests the only definition of a weed that is possible. A weed is a plant we hoe up or, rather, that we try to hoe up. A flower or a vegetable is a plant that the hoe deliberately misses. But, in spite of the hoe, the weeds have it. They survive and multiply like a subject race. . . . Well, perhaps better a weed than a geranium.

XXI

A JUROR IN WAITING

THE train was crowded with jurymen. Every one of them was saying something like " It's a disgrace," " It's a perfect scandal," " No other nation would put up with it," and " Here we all are grumbling ; and what are we going to do about it ? Nothing. That's the British way." They were not complaining of any act of injustice perpetrated against a prisoner. They were complaining of their own treatment. Fifty or sixty of them had been summoned from the four ends of the county, and kept packed away all day under a gallery at the back of the court, where there was not even room for all of them to sit down, and where there was certainly not room for all of them to breathe. It would have been an easy thing for the Clerk of the Court to choose a dozen jurymen in the first ten minutes of the day, and to dismiss the rest on their business. He might, if necessary, have also picked a reserve jury, and selected the jury for the next day's cases. The law revels in expense, however, and so a great number of middle-aged men were taken away for two whole days from their businesses and compelled to sit in filthy air and on benches that would not be endured in the gallery of a theatre, with nothing to do but watch the backs of the heads of a continuous procession of barristers and bigamists.

Few jurors would have complained, I think, if there had been any rational excuse for detaining them. What they objected to so bitterly was the fact that no use was made of them, and that they were kept there for two days, though it must have been obvious to everyone that the majority of them might as well be at home. It may be, however, that there is some great purpose underlying the present system of calling together a crowd of unnecessary jurymen. Perhaps it is a form of compulsory education for middle-aged men. It shows them the machine of the law in action, and enables them to some extent to say from their own observation whether it is being worked in a fair and humane or in a harsh and vindictive spirit. One cannot sit through one criminal case after another at the Assizes without gaining a considerable amount of material for forming a judgment on this matter. The juror in waiting, as he sees a pregnant woman swooning in the dock or a man with a high, pumpkin-shaped back to his head led off down the dark stairs to five years' penal servitude, becomes a keen critic of the British justice that may have been to him until then merely a phrase. How does British justice emerge from the test? Well, it may be that this judge was a particularly kind judge and that the policemen of this county are particularly kindly policemen, but I confess that, much as I detest other people's boasting, I came away with the impression that the boast about British justice is justified. I do not believe that it is by any means always justified in the mouths of statesmen who use it as an excuse for their own injustice, and I would not trust every judge or every jury to give a verdict free from political bias in a case that involved political issues. But in the ordinary case—"as between," in the words of the oath, "our sovereign lord the King and the prisoner at the bar"—it seems to me, if my two days' experience can be taken as typical, that British justice is not only just but merciful.

PLEASURES OF IGNORANCE

The evidence is, perhaps, insufficient, as, in most cases, the sentences were deferred. But what pleased one was the general lack of vindictiveness in the prosecution or in the police evidence. Hardly a bigamist climbed into the dock —and there was an apparently endless stream of them—to whom the local police did not give a glowing certificate of character. The chief constable of the county went into the witness-box to testify that one bigamist was "reliable," "a good worker," etc. "His general conduct," a policeman would say of another, "as regards both the women, was good." The barristers, as was natural, dwelt on the Army record of most of the men, and, even when a client had pleaded guilty, would appeal to the judge to remember that he had before him a man with a stainless past. "But wait, wait," the judge would interrupt; "you know bigamy is a very serious offence." "I quite agree with your lordship," counsel would reply nervously, "but I beg of you to take into consideration that the prisoner was carried away by his love for this woman——" This was where the judge always grew indignant. He was a little man with big eyebrows, a big nose, a big mouth, and white whiskers. His whiskers made him appear a little like Matthew Arnold in a wig and scarlet, save that he did not look as if he were sitting above the battle. "You tell me," he declared warmly, "that he loved this woman, while he admits that he deceived her into marrying him and falsely described himself in the marriage certificate as a bachelor." Counsel would again nervously agree with his lordship that his client had done wrong in deceiving the woman, but in three sentences he would have found another way round to the portraiture of the prisoner as all but a model for the young. Certainly, the great increase in the offence of bigamy proves at least the hollowness of all the talk about the growing indifference to the marriage tie. Whatever we may think of bigamists—and there are black sheep in every flock — the bigamist is manifestly a much-married man. He is a person, I should say, with the bump of domesticity excessively developed. The merely immoral man, as most of us know him, does not ask for the sanction of the law for his immorality. He does not feel the want of "a home from home," as the bigamist does. The increase in bigamy, it seems clear enough, is largely due to the war, which not only gave men opportunities for travel such as they had never had before, but enabled them to travel in a uniform which was itself a passport to many an impressionable female heart. Men had never been so much admired before. Never had they had so wide a choice of female acquaintances. " I am amazed," said Clive on a famous occasion, " at my own moderation." Many a bigamist, as he stands in the dock in these days of the cool fit, could conscientiously put forward the same plea. But the most that any of them can say is that they thought the first wife was dead or that she wanted to bring up the children Roman Catholics.

The first wife in one of the bigamy cases went into the witness-box, and I saw what to me was an incredible sight—an Englishwoman of thirty who could neither read nor write. Red-haired, tearful, weary, she did not even know the months of the year. She said a telegram had been sent to her husband saying she was dangerously ill in February. " Was that this year or last year?" asked counsel. " I don't know, sir," she said. " Come, come," said the judge, "you must know whether you were suffering from a dangerous illness this year or last." "No, sir," she replied shakily; "you see, sir, not bein' a scholar, I couldn't 'ardly tell, sir." Then a bright idea struck her. "My hospital papers could tell the date, sir." She produced from her pocket a paper saying that she had undergone an operation in a hospital in September 1919. That was all that could be got out of her. The counsel on the other side rose to cross-examine her about the dates. "You had an operation in September, you say. Were you laid up at any other time during the past two years?" "No, sir." "But you have sworn that you were ill in February, when a telegram was sent to your husband?" "Yes, sir." "And now you say that you weren't ill at any other time except in September?" "No, sir." "So you weren't ill in February?" "Oh yes, sir; I had the 'flu, sir." She was as obstinate about it all as the child in *We are Seven*. But she kept assuring us that she was no scholar. Her husband said that he had received a letter saying she was dead, and, though he had lost it, he quoted it at length "as far as he could remember it." It was a beautiful letter, expressing regret that he had not been at the side of the deathbed, where, the writer was sure, whatever faults had been on either side would have been forgiven. " You never were dead ? " the judge asked the woman. " No, sir," she replied in the same tone of *We are Seven* seriousness.

A girl was put in the dock, charged with having stolen a Post Office savings bank book. A policeman, giving evidence, said : " Until the 6th of December she was in the Wacks." " You say," said the judge, rather bewildered by the good appearance of the girl, " that she was in the workhouse ! " " In the Wacks, my lord." " I think he means the Royal Air Force," prosecuting counsel helped the judge out of his perplexity. And the word " Wraf" went from mouth to mouth round the court. The girl was guilty, but the judge told her that he was not going to send her to prison. " I don't think it would do you any good, and I don't think the interests of society call for it," he said. " What I'm going to do is to bind you over to come up for judgment if called upon. Now, go away home, and be a good girl, and, if you are, you won't hear anything more about it. You have done a very disgraceful thing, but you can live it down by good conduct in the future." There was another thief, a boy of eighteen, who had been deserted by his mother at the age of three, and whom the judge also told, though not in those words, to go and sin no more. There was also a boy who had forged his father's consent to his marriage, and he and his girl wife were lectured like children and sent home to do better in future. As the judge said to the boy : "This is not a thing you are likely to do again." His wife, who was expecting a baby, had to be carried fainting from the dock. Counsel could not bring himself to say that she was expecting a baby. He said that she was "in a certain condition." The modesty of the law is marvellous.

One of the most interesting of the prisoners was a little sleek-headed man accused of fraud, who kept moving his head about like a tortoise's out of its shell. His head was black and shining where it was not bald and shining. He had gold-rimmed spectacles and a sallow face. He glided his hands over the knobs on the front of the dock with a reptilian smoothness. He had persuaded a number of tradesmen and hotel-keepers that he was an English peer. He had even complained to one shopkeeper of the smallness of a wallet, as he needed something larger to hold the title-deeds relating to the peerage. In another case, a young man, staying in a house, had stolen, along with other things, his hostess's false teeth, her best dress, and a great quantity of underclothing. A parcel of clothing had been recovered from a second-hand shop and was shown to the lady when in the witness-box. She took up one of the garments and fingered it. "Well," said the prosecuting counsel, encouragingly, "is that your best dress?" "Naoh," she said melancholily, "that's me ypron." Then there was a young man who stole a motor-bicycle by presenting a revolver at the head of the owner. He denied that he had stolen it, and maintained that, after he had apologised to the owner "for having treated him so abruptly," they had become friendly and he had been told to take the bicycle away and pay for it later. Alas! there is a limit to human credulity. Besides, the young man had a crooked mouth. After two days in court, one begins to believe that one can tell an honest man from a liar by looking at him. Probably one is over-confident.

XXII

THE THREE-HALFPENNY BIT

As a rule, there is nothing that offends us more than a new kind of money. We felt humiliated in the early days of the war when we were no longer paid in heavy little discs of gold, and had to accept paper pounds and ten-shillingses. We even sneered at the design. We always sneer at the design of new money or a new stamp. But we hated the paper even more than the design. We could not believe it had any value. We spent it as though it were paper. One would as soon have thought of collecting old newspapers as of playing the miser with it. That is probably the true secret of the fall in the value of money. Economists explain it in other ways. But it seems likeliest that paper money lost its value because we did not value it. Shopkeepers took advantage of our foolish innocence, and the tailor demanded sums in paper that he would never have dared to ask in gold. I doubt if the habit of thrift will ever be restored till the gold currency comes back. Gold is the only metal for which human beings have any lasting respect. No one but a child would save up pennies. There is something in gold—the colour, perhaps, reminding us of the sun, the god of our ancestors —that puts us into the mood of worshippers. The children of Israel found it impossible not to worship the golden calf. They have gone on worshipping it ever since. Had the calf been of paper, they would, I feel confident, have remained good Christians.

The influence of hatred on the expenditure of money is seen in our attitude to threepenny bits. Nine out of ten people feel sincerely indignant when a threepenny bit is given to them in their change. The shopkeeper who gives you two threepenny bits instead of a sixpence knows this and, as he hands you the money, says apologetically : " Do you mind ? " You say : " Not at all," but you do. You know that they will be a constant misery to you till you get rid of them. You know that if you give one of them to a bus conductor, even if he is able to restrain himself, he will feel like throwing you off the top of the bus. When at length you spend one of them in a post office—one never has the same scruples about Government institutions—you hurry out with a guilty air, not having dared to look the lady at the counter in the eye. In the nineteenth century, when people went to church, they used to get rid of their threepenny bits at the collection. They at once relieved themselves of a nuisance, and enjoyed the luxury of flinging the gleam of silver on to the plate. Many a good Baptist has trusted to his threepenny bit's being mistaken for a sixpence, by the neighbours, at least—perhaps even by Heaven. He has a notion that the widow's mite was a threepenny bit, and feels that his gift is in a great tradition.

The popular hatred of certain coins, however, goes back to a far earlier date than the invention of the threepenny bit. Even gold, when it was first introduced into the English coinage, was met with such a storm of denunciation that it had to be withdrawn. This was in the time of Henry III., who issued a golden penny to take the place of the silver penny that had hitherto been the chief English coin.

PLEASURES OF IGNORANCE

It was only in the reign of Edward III. that gold coins became established in England. They may have helped to recommend themselves to the nation by their intensely anti-French character. They bore the French arms, and announced that King Edward was King of England and France. France is a country lying close to the shores of England, and is of great strategic importance to her. I do not know whether the copper coins which first came into England in the time of Charles II. raised any clamour of public protest. The nation, I fancy, was so relieved to get back to cakes and ale that it was not inclined to be censorious about the new halfpennies and farthings. In the old days, people had made their own halfpennies and farthings by the simple process of cutting pennies into halves and quarters. They also issued private coins on the same principle on which we nowadays write cheques. Municipalities and shopkeepers alike issued these tokens, or promises to pay, and without them there would not have been sufficient currency for the transaction of business. The copper coins of Charles II. were intended to put a stop to this unofficial sort of

money, but towards the end of the eighteenth
century there was such a scarcity of copper
currency that local shopkeepers and bankers
defied the law and again began to issue their
own coins. I have in my possession what looks
like a George III. shilling, with the King's
head on one side and, on the other, inside a
wreath of shamrocks, the inscription: "Bank
Token, 10 Pence Irish, 1813." It was turned
up by the plough on a Staffordshire farm a few
years ago. Speaking of this reminds me that
a separate Irish coinage continued even after
the Union of 1800. It was not till 1817 that
English gold and silver became current in
Ireland, and Irish pennies and halfpennies
were struck as late as the reign of George IV.
The Scottish coins came to an end more than
a century earlier. The name of one of them,
however, the "bawbee," has survived in popular
humour. Some people say that the name is
merely a corruption of "baby," referring to
the portrait of Queen Mary as an infant. It
seems to me as unlikely a derivation as could
be imagined.

Of all the English coins, the first appearance
of which occasioned popular anger, none had

a worse reception than the two-shilling piece, which appeared in 1849. " This piece," says Miss G. B. Rawlings in *Coins and How to Know Them*, a book rich in information, " was unfavourably received, owing to the omission of ' Dei Gratia' after the Queen's name, and was stigmatised as the godless or graceless florin." The florin, however, so called after a Florentine coin, had come to stay, but since 1851 it has been as godly in inscription as any of the other money in one's pocket. The coin has survived, but hardly the name. One can with an effort call a spade a spade, but who would think of calling a florin a florin ? The coin itself for a time bore the inscription : " One Florin, Two Shillings," as though the name called for translation. Since the introduction of the florin, there have been many coins that aroused popular hatred. The four-shilling piece, especially, that was struck in the year of Queen Victoria's Jubilee, was received with a howl of execration. Men went about in constant dread of argument with shopkeepers as to whether they had given them a four-shilling or a five-shilling piece. In the interests of the national good temper the coin ceased to be struck after

THE THREE-HALFPENNY BIT

1890. Englishmen, however, disliked the entire Jubilee coinage. They disliked the Queen's portrait, and they disliked especially a sixpence which could be easily gilded to look like a half-sovereign. The sixpences were hurriedly withdrawn, but schoolboys continued to treasure them in the belief that they were worth fabulous sums. Like groats, the delight of one's childhood, they began to be desirable as soon as they ceased to be common. When King Edward VII. came to the throne, there was another outburst of hatred of new money. The chief objection to it was that the King's effigy had been designed by a German and had not even been designed well. It was at this time, perhaps, when people began to hate the money in their pockets, that the reign of modern extravagance began. To get rid of a sovereign bearing a design by Herr Fuchs seemed a patriotic duty. Thrift and pro-Germanism were indistinguishable.

Much as men detest new sorts of money in their own country, however, many of us take a childish pleasure on our first arrival in France in handling strange and unfamiliar coins. One of the great pleasures of travel is changing

one's money. There is a certain lavishness
about the coinage of the Continent that appeals
to our curiosity. Even in getting a five-franc
piece we never know whether it will bear the
emblem of a republic, a kingdom or an empire.
Coins of Greece and Italy jingle in our pocket
with those of the impostor, Louis Napoleon,
and those of the wicked Leopold, King of the
Belgians. In Switzerland I remember even
getting a Cretan coin, which I was humiliated
by being unable to pass at a post office. The
postal official took down a huge diagram
containing pictures of all the European coins
he was allowed to accept. He studied Greek
coins and, for all I know, Jugo-Slav coins, but
nowhere could he find the image of the coin I
had proffered him. Crete for him did not exist.
He shook his head solemnly and handed the
coin back. Is there any situation in which a
man feels guiltier than when his money is thrust
back on him as of no value? This happens
oftener, perhaps, in France than in any other
country. France has the reputation of being
the country of bad money. The reputation is,
I believe, exaggerated, though I have known
a Boulogne tram conductor to refuse even a

THE THREE-HALFPENNY BIT

50-centime piece as bad. I remember vividly a warning given to me on this subject during my first visit to France. I was sitting with a friend in an estaminet in a small village in the north of France, when an English chauffeur insinuated himself into the conversation. He was eager to give us advice about France and the French. " I like the French," he said, " but you can't trust them. Look out for bad money. They're terrors for bad money. I'd have been done oftener myself, only that luckily I married a Frenchwoman. She's in the ticket office at the Maison des Délits—you probably know the name—it's a dancing-hall in Montmartre. Any time I get a bad 5-franc piece, I pass it on to her, and she gets rid of it in the change to some Froggie. My God, they *are* dishonest! I wouldn't say a word against the French, but just that one thing. They're dishonest—damned dishonest." He sat back on the bench, a figure of insular rectitude but of cosmopolitan broadminded-ness. Is it not the perfect compromise?

XXIII

THE MORALS OF BEANS

" Nine bean-rows will I have there," cries Mr
Yeats in describing his Utopia in *The Lake Isle
of Innisfree.* I have only two. They run east
to west between the second-early potatoes and
the red-currant bushes. They are broad beans.
They are in flower just now, and every flower
is a little black-and-white butterfly. That,
however, is the good side of the account. If
you look closer at them, you will see that each
of them appears as if its head had been dipped
into coal-dust. There is a congregation of the
blackest of all insects hiding in horrid con-
gestion among the leaves and flowers at the
top. Compared to them, the green-fly on the
roses has almost charm. There is something
slummy and unwashed-looking about the black
blight. These insects are as foul as a stagnant
pond. Though they have wings, they seem
incapable of flight. They are microbes of a

THE MORALS OF BEANS

larger growth—a disease and a desecration.
On the other hand, there is one good point
about them : they are very stupid. Instead
of spreading themselves out along the entire
extent of the bean and so lessening their peril,
they mass themselves in hordes in the very
tops of the plants as though they had all some
passionate taste for rocking in the wind like
the baby on the tree-top. This is what gives
the gardener his opportunity. He has but to
walk along the rows, pinching off the top of
each plant, and filling his flat little basket
(called, I believe, a trug) with them, and lo,
the beans are safe, and produce all the finer
and fuller pods as a result of their having been
stunted.

At this point the moral thrusts out its head.
There are those who believe that beans have
no morals. To call a man "Old bean" gives
him, it is said, a pleasant feeling that he is
something of a dog. Gilbert, again, in *Patience*
has a reference to "a not-too-French French
bean" that suggests a ribald estimate of this
family of plants. The broad bean, on the
other hand, seems to me to exude morality—
not least, when it parts with its head to save

its life. There is no better preacher in the vegetable garden. It is the very Chrysostom of the gospel of frustration—the gospel that a great loss may be a great gain—the gospel that through their repressions men may all the more successfully achieve their ends.

Nor is this gospel confined to the sect of the beans (which are by a happy paradox both broad and evangelical). The apple-trees bear the same message in their unpruned branches —unpruned owing to a long absence from home during the winter. It is an amazing fact—I speak as an amateur—but it is an amazing fact, if it is a fact, that an apple-tree, if it is left to itself, will not grow apples. It has an entirely selfish purpose in life. Its aim is to be a tree, living to itself, producing a multitude of shoots and leaves. It succeeds in living a rich and fruitful life only when the gardener has come with the abhorrèd shears and lopped its branches till it must feel like a frustrate thing. The fruit is the fruit of frustration. Were it not for this frustration, it would ultimately return to a state of wildness, and would become a crabbed and barren weed, fit only to be a perch for birds.

THE MORALS OF BEANS

Thus, it seems to me, the broad bean and the apple-tree are persuasive defenders of civilisation and of those concomitants of civilisation—morality and the arts. Heretics frequently arise, both in ethics and in the arts, who say: "No more restraints! Give the bean its head." There are psycho-analysts who appear to regard frustration as the one serious evil in life, and the apostles of *vers libre* denounce metre and rhyme because these merely serve to frustrate the natural impulses of the imagination. As a matter of fact, it is this very frustration that gives poetry much of its depth and vehemence. Great genius expresses itself, not in the freedom of formlessness, but in the limitations of form. Shakespeare's passion turned instinctively to the most frustrative of all poetic forms—that of the sonnet—in order to express itself in perfection. It is, as a rule, those who have nothing to say who wish to say it without the terrible frustrations of form. Obviously, there is a golden mean in the arts as in all things, and there comes a point at which form passes into formalism. Genius requires just enough frustration to increase its vehemence, and so to transmute nature into art. It is possible that some frustration of a comparable kind is needed in order to transmute nature into morality, and that the man who would, in Milton's phrase, make of his life a poem must submit to commandments as difficult as those of metre or rhyme. It is not merely the Christians and the Stoics who have maintained this ; Epicurus himself was a believer in virtue as a means to happiness. This, indeed, is a commonplace written all over the face of nature. There is no great happiness without opposition except for children. The climber struggles with the hill, the rower with the water, the digger with the earth. They are all men who live on the understanding that the pleasures of difficulty are greater even than the pleasures of ease.

The biographies of famous men are prolific of examples that support the theory of frustration. Homer, they say, was blind, and the legend seems to suggest that his blindness, far from injuring, abetted his genius. Tyrtæus, being physically unable to fight, became the poet of fighting, and achieved more with his words than did most men with their weapons. Demosthenes, again, was an orator frustrated

THE MORALS OF BEANS

by many defects. Everyone knows the story
of his wretched articulation and how he shut
himself up and practised speaking with pebbles
in his mouth in order to overcome it. Few of
the great orators, indeed, seem to have suc-
ceeded in oratory without difficulty. Neither
Cicero nor Burke spoke with the natural ease
of many a young man in a Y.M.C.A. debating
society. And the great writers, like the great
orators, have been, in many instances, men
doomed in some important respect to lead
frustrated lives. Mr Beerbohm recently said
that he has never known a man of genius
whose life was not marred by some obvious
defect. People have talked for two thousand
years of the desirability of *mens sana in corpore
sano*, but if everybody possessed this—possessed
it from birth and without effort—there would
probably soon be a shortage of genius. The
sanity of genius is not the sanity of the
healthy minded athlete : it is the sanity of
the human spirit struggling against forces that
threaten to frustrate it. The greatest love-
poetry has not been written by men who have
found easy happiness in love. Donne's poems
are the poems of a frustrated lover. Keats's

greatest poetry was the fruit of unfulfilled love. Thus genius turns poverty into riches. Few men of genius are enviable save in their genius. Beethoven, a frustrate lover and ultimately a deaf musician, is a type of genius at its most sublime.

Charles Lamb, as we read the *Essays*, seems at times to be one of the most enviable of men, but that is only because he is supremely lovable. Who knows how much we owe to the defects of his life? Even the impediment in his speech seems to have been one of the conditions of his genius. He tells us that, if he had not stammered, he would probably have been a clergyman, and, if he had been a clergyman, he would hardly have been Elia. His life, too, was that of a tragic bachelor—he whose writings breathe the finest spirit of fireside comedy. There could be no better example of the truth that genius is, as a rule, a response to apparently hostile limitations.

On the whole, then, the common-sense attitude to life is, not to deplore one's limitations, but to make the best of them. No man need envy another his good fortune too bitterly. Good fortune has wasted as many men as it has assisted. George Wyndham was one of the most fortunate men of his time—strong, handsome, an athlete, an orator, a statesman, a writer with a sense of style, popular, rich, and with nine out of ten of the attributes that we envy most. Had achievement come less easily to him, he might have been a greater man. There have been ugly men who have been more enviable. There have been weedy men who were more enviable. There have been poor men who were more enviable. But the truth is, one does not know whom to envy. It is probably wise to envy nobody.

It would be foolish, however, to pretend that frustration is a desirable thing in itself, apart from all other considerations. The beans nod their heads to no such gospel. Frustration may easily reach the point of destruction. One might frustrate one's broad beans excessively by pulling them up by the roots or cutting them down to within an inch of the ground. There must still be room left for the life of the plant to find a new outlet. The beans do not preach a sermon against liberty, but only against lawlessness. But, for all I know, they may preach different gospels to different amateur gardeners. Each of us finds in nature what he wishes to find. I confess I myself am prejudiced in favour of sermons of a consoling kind. It is consoling to think that, in a world of defects, a defect often carries with it its own compensation—that strength, as the preachers say, may be made perfect in weakness. But, when one looks round and enumerates the miseries of human beings, one wonders how far this is, after all, true except for men whose gifts are naturally greater than hog, dog or devil can imperil.

XXIV

ON SEEING A JOKE

ALMOST any man can make a joke, but it sometimes requires a clever man to see one. It is
said that a Scotsman "jokes wi' deeficulty."
What we really mean is that it is often difficult
to see a Scotsman's jokes or even to know
whether he is joking or being serious. As a
matter of fact, the Scots are an unusually
humorous race. They make jokes, however,
with the long faces of undertakers, and one is
sometimes afraid to laugh for fear of appearing
frivolous on a solemn occasion. I have in
mind one brilliant Scottish professor who,
whether he is jocular or serious, invariably
monologises in the tones of a man condoling
with a widow. He half-shuts his eyes and
folds his hands, and, for the first minute or two,
takes an evil delight in leaving you in doubt
whether he is launching into a tragic narrative
or whether he will suddenly look up through

his spectacles and expect to see you laughing. His English friends are in a constant state of embarrassment because they know that he is a humorist of genius, but his humour is so subtle that they do not trust themselves to see the point when it comes and laugh at the right place. Now, there are only two things that can make the professor look sterner than he looks while giving birth to a joke. One is, if you laugh too early : the other is, if the great moment comes and you don't laugh at all. He makes no complaint, but he sits back in his chair, looking like an embittered owl. And everybody else in the room has a sense of ghastly failure—his own failure, not the professor's. To miss seeing a joke is, in some circumstances, far worse than to miss making the point of a joke visible. If one were in the position of a Queen Victoria, one might, of course, quench the professor by merely saying : "We are not amused." But even Queen Victoria, when she said this, did not mean that she had not seen the joke but that she had seen it and didn't like it.

It is not only the subtle and Scottish jokes, however, that are at times difficult to see with the naked eye. There is also the joke that

hits you in the eye like a blow and blinds you.
Captain Wedgwood Benn referred to a joke of
this kind in the House of Commons on the
authority of Mr Stephen Gwynn. A judge of
the Irish High Court, he related, was recently
travelling on a tram which was held up by
Black-and-Tans. The Black-and-Tans, who,
like the Most High, are no respecters of
persons, called on the judge to descend, using
the quaint colloquial formula: "Come down,
you Irish bastard; put up your hands."
Captain Wedgwood Benn does not unfortunately possess a twentieth-century sense of
humour, and he did not see this particular joke.
The comedy of a judge's being addressed as an
Irish bastard did not strike him. I doubt if
half-a-dozen members of the House of Commons
realised the beauty of the joke till Sir Hamar
Greenwood got up and explained it. "I
happen to know the judge," said the twinkling
Chief Secretary. "He told the story himself
with great glee, and here it is. Mr Justice
Wylie, the last, and one of the best judges
appointed in Ireland, was riding on a tramcar
to a hunting meet. When he got to the end
of his ride, there were some policemen on duty,

and they did use a word which, I trust, no hon. Member of this House will ever use, in calling him down from the tram. They did him no harm. He treated it as a joke, and he would be the man most surprised to find it quoted in the House and in the *Observer* as an example of the decadence of the Irish police." I agree with Sir Hamar. A joke is a joke, and many Irishmen, unlike Mr Justice Wylie, are unduly thin-skinned. The only criticism I would make on Sir Hamar Greenwood's idea of a joke is that he appears to suggest that it would have been less funny if the Black-and-Tans had done the judge some harm. I should have expected him rather to dilate on the attractions of life in the Irish police force for men with a sense of humour. Suppose the judge had been robbed of his watch, or had had his front teeth broken with the muzzle of a revolver like the University Professor at Cork, would not that have made the incident still funnier? Suppose he had been carried round as a hostage on a motor-lorry, or shot with a bucket over his head, as has happened to other innocent men, would it not have been a theme for Aristophanes, who got so much fun out of

the idea of one person's being beaten in mistake
for another?

I am confident that distinguished Englishmen
will behave in the spirit of Mr Justice Wylie,
when there is an outbreak of humour among
the English police. Mr Justice Darling will,
no doubt, enjoy himself hugely on the day on
which an armed policeman first holds up his
motor-car, and addresses him: "'Ullo, you
blasted old Bolshevik, come off the perch, and
quick about it, and put up the 'Idden 'And!"
There are some judges who would complain to
the Home Office, if such a thing happened to
them. Mr Justice Darling, however, has a
keen sense of humour. I feel certain that
on arriving in Court after his experiences he
would tell the story with great glee. He
would turn up his face sideways, as he does
when he is amused, and say to the jury: "A
most amusing thing happened to me this
morning, by the way . . ." There is no end,
indeed, to the directions in which a police force
saturated with the Greenwoodian sense of fun
might add to the gaiety of nations. They
might arm themselves with squirts, and laughing Cabinet ministers would have to duck as

they passed down Whitehall in order to avoid a drenching. Pluffing peas at the bishops on their way to the House of Lords would also be good sport, so long as they did not really hurt any of them. To bash the Lord Chancellor's hat over his eyes would be going too far, as it involves a money loss, but a harmless blow on the crown with a bladder would be rather amusing. It would also be amusing if a number of policemen were told off to greet Mr Lloyd George with cries of " Welsh attorney," and to chaff him with genial scurrilities on his arrival at the House. If these things happened, there are killjoys, I know, who would immediately set up a clamour for the restoration of discipline in the police force. Mr Lloyd George, however, has always been a man who can not only make a joke but take one, and I am sure that he at least would defend the democratic right of the policeman to a bit of chaff.

Nor would I confine the right of chaff to the police force. I would make it universal. I should like to see it introduced into the Church itself. Even the dullest sermon would become entertaining if the verger had the right and the habit of interpolating such remarks

as: "Cheese it, Pussyfoot!" or "Ring off, you
bleedin' old bore, ring off!" There has been
too little of this sort of popular raillery in recent
years. The bus-drivers used to be past masters
at it, poking their quiet fun impartially at
their fellow-drivers and ordinary citizens.
Whether it is that the drivers of motor-buses
realise that no joke could be heard above the
din, or whether it is that they feel as ill-
tempered as they look, their arrival has made
fatal inroads on the geniality of London. An
artist with uncut hair can still awaken a spark
of the old wit if he goes down a back street,
and women and children will revive for his
benefit the venerable witticism: "Get your
hair cut!" But, generally speaking, there has
been a notable decline in the humours of insult
within living memory. The Germans, always
fond of a joke, made an effort to revive it
during the war. It was a common thing for
them, we are told, on capturing a prisoner, to
address him as "Schweinhund" or "Ver-
dammte Engländer," or by some other good-
humoured phrase of the same kind. I regret
to say that some Englishmen were so deficient
in the sense of humour that, instead of taking

this in the spirit in which it was offered, they bitterly resented it. I cannot, indeed, recall a single instance of an Englishman who properly appreciated the joke of being called a "Schwein-hund" by a man he had never seen before. You will seek in vain through the literature of prisoners of war for a returned soldier who tells the story of the names he was called with the glee that it deserves. And yet, no doubt, the Germans enjoyed the joke thoroughly, and would have been surprised to find it quoted in the *Observer* as an example of the decadence of the German Army.

Perhaps, however, the " Schweinhund " joke does not afford an entirely fair comparison. It is a simple joke, whereas in the Greenwood joke there are two elements. There is the element of insult, and there is the element of mistaken identity. It is not merely that some-body or other was called " You Irish bastard," but that the wrong person was called " You Irish bastard." Thus, if a policeman addressed a woman in Oxford Street in the words : " 'Op it, you old bitch," it would be only mildly funny, if the woman were a poor woman. But it would be immensely funny if she turned out to be a marchioness. The marchioness, no doubt, would be enchanted, and would tell the story with great glee. If she were a sentimentalist, she might say to herself: "Is this really the way in which ordinary human beings are treated by the police? This is a hideous state of affairs in which bullies in uniform are allowed to address foul insults to whom they please. Thank heaven, it has happened to someone like me. Now, I can tell the Home Secretary, and he will put an end to the whole system." One never knows what a modern Home Secretary might do, but I doubt if one could be found who would reply to the marchioness: "Well, he did you no harm. You know, to me it all seems rather funny." And yet most things have their funny side if you look on them in the right spirit. It would have been a funny thing if the hangman had executed the wrong prisoner instead of Crippen. The hanged man would not have seen the joke, but impartial onlookers would have seen it, and Crippen would have seen it. Similarly, if a drunken man threw a brick at his wife and hit the missionary by mistake, who could help laughing? Even the wife, if she had a sense of humour, would have to join in. Over-sensitive souls, such as Shelley was, might view the incident with pain and mourn over a world in which human beings treated each other in such a way. But life is a hard school, and it is not well to be over-sensitive. After all, if we all became angels, there would be no jokes left. We should have no clowns in the music-halls—no comic boxing-turns with glorious thumpings on unexpecting noses. Heaven is a place without laughter because there is no cruelty in it—no insults and no accidents. As for us, we are children of earth, and may as well enjoy the advantages of our position. So let us laugh, " Ha, ha ! "—let us laugh, " Ho, ho ! "

The world is so full of a number of things,
I'm sure we should all be as happy as kings.

And never was it so full of a number of things as since a Coalition Government came into power — queer, delightful things, for instance, like policemen who call judges "bastard," as who should say : " Cheerio, old thing ! " Our grandfathers would not have seen that joke. That is one of the things that convince me of the reality of progress.

XXV

GOING TO THE DERBY

"Do they have as much fun at the Derby as they used to?" I heard an old gentleman in a white hat, canary gloves, and buttoned boots asking a fellow-passenger in a London train. Fun? No; one would hardly call it that. Looking back on it after forty years one will no doubt call it fun. But it is certainly not fun while it lasts.

The two most important features of the Derby are getting there and getting away again. Getting there is harder work than bricklaying or journalism. You may ride in a motor-car, but your motor will be as useless to you as a submarine in a swimming bath. From Sutton to Epsom and from Epsom to the Downs a long procession of motor-cars, buses, waggonettes, greengrocers' carts, lorries, school carts, drays, and human beings stretches like a serpent of infinite length—a serpent that is apparently too sick to move. One thinks of it as an old serpent that has made itself very ill by swallowing machinery.

Every few minutes it gives the machinery in its inward parts a shake, and makes one more effort to crawl. A queer rattle, shiver, and groan run through it from tip to tail. But the effort is too much for it. It immediately subsides on a lame and impotent stomach, and hour after hour passes with no other diversion except the antics of an occasional nervous horse that rises on his hind legs and waves his forefeet in the back of your neck over the hood of the motor.

There is a common belief that the crowd that goes to the Derby is a cheerful crowd —that it sings and plays concertinas and changes hats. There could not be a greater delusion. It is as quiet and determined as a procession of men and women going to hear Dr Horton preaching at Hampstead. Not a song—well, one song. Not a joke—well, one joke, when a fat man saw a poor brown lop-eared ass in a field of daisies, and called out: "There's the winner o' the Durby!" He apparently felt it was a very good joke, for he repeated it to parties on the tops of buses and parties on greengrocers' carts and parties in furniture vans.

The sun, however, was unpropitious for jokes. Even the East Ender, who had worked an edging of red and white wool into his pony's mane and hung rosettes of red, white, and blue at its ears, was too busy perspiring and hating his hundred thousand neighbours to smile. He was also busy weighing his chances of getting to Epsom Downs before Judgment Day. I admired his spirit in waving a whip with a knot of coloured ribbons. There was little other colour to be seen. We were a procession of victims—red as beef, steaming like the window of a fried-fish shop, dusty, swollen-veined—and we could only sink back helpless and gasping in the grip of the monstrous procession of wheeled things that advanced more slowly than any snail that was ever known on this side of the Ural Mountains.

I doubt if that procession ever reached Epsom Downs. I did so only because I got out and walked; and even then the first two races were over. Half England seemed already to have arrived on the hills, and to have pitched its wigwams there. The other half was blocking up the road for ten miles back, and could not possibly arrive in time for the Derby; but the half who had arrived had already set up a city of booths and flags on hill after hill as far as the eye could see.

There may have been encampments of this vastness in the days of Xerxes, but surely never since. It was oppressive, overwhelming. There were so many people there that there was no room for anybody. There was no room, so far as I could see, for the man who plays the three-card trick on the top of an open umbrella, or for the man with the tape and pencil, and even the beggars who prayed by the roadside for your success were few. There was simply a crush—an enormous, sweltering, and appallingly silent crush. Even the bookmakers seemed to be awed by it. They stood on their stands beside blackboards full of horses' names and mystical figures, but they did not yell at you hoarsely, bullyingly, as bookmakers ought to do. If, having looked at the elephantine portrait advertisement of one of them, you wished to bet with him, he would consent in a listless way, and say wearily to his clerk: "Nine-nine-one, seventy shillings to a dollar Polumetis," as he handed you a blue, red, and green card.

I do not blame him for not being enthusiastic. I am myself no longer enthusiastic about Polumetis. Still, one wished for a little violence besides the violence of the sun and of the man who tried to sell you a shilling's worth of sausage and who said he was " the only firm, the only firm in the place." Camden Town on a Saturday night could give points to Derby Day for colour and uproar. Derby Day is so big, perhaps, that it is frightened of itself.

But I forgot. There was one violent man. He was fat, hatless, and sweating, and he was hoarse with shouting superlatives about his tips to a circle of poor old men, " dunchers " in caps, small boys in jerseys, and tired-looking country girls.

" If only I could tell you where I got my information," he declared, " you'd—you'd be s'prised. If any of you has got twenty-five pahnd abaht him—if you've got even a tenner —why, if you've only got ten bob—well, you can't exactly have a gamble for ten bob, but you can 'ave a bit o' fun, anyway. If you take my advice—it's 'ere on this bit o' paper—

you can 'ave it for a bob—I can give you three
'orses that'll turn your ten bob into a tenner—
see? Some people tell you Tetratema's going
to win."

He made a face of disgust, popularly known
as giving Tetratema the raspberry. "Don't
you believe it. Didn't I tell you Tagrag?
Didn't I tell you Arion? 'Ere, take my tip,
and you'll dance all the w'y 'ome with joy to-
night. Dance? Why, you'll go 'ome jazzin'
all the w'y."

And he spread out his fat hands and threw
out his fat stomach, and danced on the grass,
just to show one how one ought to behave if
one backed a Derby winner.

Meanwhile, his partner, dressed as a red and
white jockey, in a peaked cap and incongruous
puttees, moved round the circle thrusting his
slips of tips almost angrily on us. "Go on,"
he ordered us. "What's a bob to a gambler?
You people read the papers and believe what
you see in 'em. The papers! I tell you
stryte—the worst pack of rogues and bookmakers in England." A simple old man of
ninety, who had lost his teeth, beckoned to him
and paid him a shilling for his tip. The jockey

took him aside and whispered impressively into his ear. Then he said, in a loud voice: "Are you satisfied, sir?" "Quite satisfied," quavered the old man. I wish I could have stayed near him. I should like to have seen him jazzing later in the evening.

Sausages, lemonade, fried fish, chewing gum, bets, ladies standing on the roofs of taxis, a try-your-strength machine, extemporised conveniences of civilisation, with youths standing by them and yelling "Commodytion!" hills of humanity in all attitudes of dazedness and despair, the thunder and the shouting of the distant bookmakers under the stands, the quiet of the ten thousand free-lance book-makers who were, I suppose, breaking the law in the open spaces; the dust, the sun, the smell, faces smeary with fruit, the cunning tinker in an old khaki hat with striped ribbon, who was selling some twopenny instrument that was supposed to imitate either the bark of a dog or the song of a nightingale—one could not tell which from the noise he made with it; stand after stand packed to the sky with what are called serried ranks of human beings, who looked like immense banks of many-coloured shingle, and who, as they raised a million pairs of field-glasses to two million eyes, scintillated in the distance like a bank of shingle after a wave has broken on it on a tropical noon—it was certainly an amazing medley of spectacle and odour.

It is said that an important horse-race took place. It is even said that Polumetis ran in it. I looked for him everywhere—over people's heads, under people's heads, through motor-buses, round the corners of refreshment tents, in the sky above, and on the earth beneath. But no Polumetis was to be seen anywhere—except on my race-card, where I read about his lilac-coloured jockey. A jockey in lilac—how beautiful, how Japanese! And, indeed, all the jockeys as they paraded down the field before the race seemed to have robbed a rainbow.

They brought meaning and beauty into an otherwise bald and unconvincing mob. I assure you I love horse-racing—if I could see it. But of all the people who congregated the little crooked hills of Epsom, I doubt if ten people in a hundred saw it. You knew that

the horses had started only because, as you lay
dreaming, the million people on the stands
suddenly made you jump with a loud, sharp,
and terrifying bark, which said: "They're off!"
in one syllable.

Then there was deep silence, and somebody
near me said: "The favourite can't be leading,
or they would be shouting." Then from the
stands came a murmur like bees, a muttering
as of a man talking in his sleep, a growling as
of wind in a cave. This only served to inten-
sify the silence of a defeated people. One
knew that something awful must be happening.
Perhaps even Polumetis was winning.

Above the heads of the crowd the heads of
jockeys began to be visible. A fool cried out:
"The favourite wins." Another: "Allenby has
it." Then one had a glimpse of three horses
close—well, fairly close—on each other's tails,
and none of them the grey Tetratema. I
noticed that on one of them crouched a jockey
in exquisite grass-green. He passed like a fine
phrase out of a poem of which one does not
know the rest. But I did not really know
who had won till the numbers were put up
on the board. Then a badly shaven man in a

bowler cried : " Spion Kop has won ! Bravo ! " and clapped his friend on the back. The rest of us looked at him with contempt. The tinker-nosed man who played the instrument that sang like a dog or barked like a nightingale began to squeak it into people's ears.

The crowd began pouring itself through itself, and the dust from its feet rose like a cloud till it was difficult to see across the course.

And the motor-car broke down on the way home.

And Polumetis didn't win.

And I'm as tired as a dog. . . .

And so say all of us.

XXVI

THIS BLASTED WORLD

EVERYTHING has begun to have a blasted look till the sun shines. The ferns have been beaten down by the wind and the rain, and lie withered and broken-backed among the brambles, waiting till some poor man thinks it worth his while to go off with a load of them on his back for bedding. The brambles, too, all hoops and arches, have the air of dying things, though white blossoms still continue to appear, and the fruit is not yet all ripened and many of the leaves are as red and bright as flowers. The edges of most of the leaves have began to crumple : they are victims of a creeping sickness that eats into them and dirties them, and makes bramble and fern together an inextricable wilderness of refuse.

This, however, is only if one looks too closely. The hill that loses itself among the rocks on the sea-shore is capped and patched with just such refuse as this, but how happily

the rust-colour of dying things is broken by
the grey of the loose stone walls—" hedges,"
they call them in Cornwall—that seem to totter
up the hill like old men! The mist of rain
that leaves each individual plant bedraggled
seems to make the red and green and grey
pattern of the patched hill only more beautiful
and mysterious. The truth is, winter speaks
with two voices even in these early days. She
has one voice that sends cold shivers down our
backs. She has another voice that is refreshment like water from a spring. She speaks
with the first voice in the crooked trees. In
the summer they were cloaked and glorious.
Now, when their cloaks seem so much more
necessary, they are left naked, poor creatures,
their backs to the sea-wind, with the air of
runaways unable to escape. They seem bent
and poised for flight, but when a blast of wind
comes and tugs at them they are as the stump
of a tooth that will not move, and the leaves
(such of them as are left), which in summer
made a music as pleasant as that of windbells,
rattle in their branches like the laughter of a
skeleton. The oak and the thorn-bush could
scarcely writhe more if they were crippled by

rheumatism. Every leaf on the sycamore is spotted as if with some foul black acid.

Here, too, however, as soon as the leaves have fallen, the world is restored to cheerfulness. The withering tree seems a sufferer. The fallen leaf is an imp, an adventurer. As the wind sweeps round a bend in the road, leaf after leaf is up and performing cart-wheels down the road as if Christmas Day had come. Thousands of them, borne along in a dance of this kind, advance with the beflustered, orderly air of a procession of starlings. The world ceases to be a universal grave. It is at the very least a dance and a dust-storm.

There are some days, no doubt, on which the chill damp in the air seems to terrify almost every living thing into hiding, and the stillness of the dead world is not disturbed by any bird or insect. Even the jackdaws have mysteriously disappeared like melted snow. But no sooner does the storm in the sky break up into floating islands of cloud and the sun shine than all the world begins to glitter again, bramble and ivy and stone, and a host of tiny and coloured creatures resume their game of an infinite general post in the bright air. The ivy especially is a little continent of life where-ever it grows. Clambering over a wall or climbing up among the sloes in a blackthorn it attracts bee and wasp and fly, blue fly and grey fly and green fly, to graze on the pollen of its late flowers. The ivy is the last of the plants to flower, and insects come to it as from the ends of the earth in rejoicing myriads. Among the berries in the hedges the birds, too, rejoice. The robin, though for the most part, I believe, a meat-eater, becomes unambiguously happy at this time of year. He has usurped the morning, and, while one is lying in bed, he is boasting in the trees outside where the thrush and the blackbird will in a few months be boasting with their scarcely more beautiful voices. I am half persuaded that his song becomes different at this season. As he sits and sways on the top of a cypress and looks down on a rich and eatable world, he seems to have cast every note of pensive sadness out of his being and to sing aloud the rapture of a happy stomach. He is no longer the singer of elegy but of ecstasy. He is as unlike his old simple, friendly, appealing, pathetic self as a beggar who has come into a fortune. He actually swaggers, and, as he does so, he can fill a garden or a wood at the end of October with the pleasure of spring.

The large titmouse in its dark cap, and the blue-tit, almost too pretty for an English winter in its blue and yellow coat, also hasten to the feast of the berries. I do not know whether, under the iron reign of high prices, people have ceased to hang out coco-nuts in their gardens for the blue-tits; at present, fortunately, the berries are abundant, and it is pleasant to see a tit venture to the edge of the road in quest of one and then fly off into hiding, like a thief, with a red ball in his beak. A scarcely less pretty bird that one sees flying across the road now and then with cries of alarm is the grey wagtail. The grey wagtail, you probably know, is the wagtail that is not grey. As it struggles and shrills through the sunny air, it seems a delight mainly of yellow. Both its cries and its flight make one think that it lives in constant terror of falling. It proceeds through the air in a series of efforts and ups-and-downs, and its long tail seems perpetually to threaten to misguide it into collapse. Down among the rocks and in the fields near them, the real grey wagtails abound—the pied wagtails, as they are called —with their white cheeks and their less hysterical voices that greet one in passing with a pleasant little " Cheerio ! " As they alight from the air beside a puddle, they indulge in a little prance as though they were trying to cut a figure of eight on nothing or were essaying in some manner to sweep their tails out of way. Their whole existence, however, is a dance. Whether they pick their food from the rocks or in a field of cows, the alert head and jerking tail are never still, but are nervously ready for flight almost before the hint of danger. And they have usually with them as nervous companions the rock-pipits, charming little tight-skinned, low-crowned birds that hurry off wavily through the air, reiterating their solitary note of fear as they fly.

The starlings, which seemed to disappear for a time, have now returned to the fields near the sea. They have left their wonderful sheen somewhere behind them, and are mottled and plebeian. Still, to see a cloud of them alighting in a field at the end of a swift circle of flight is a pretty enough spectacle.

THIS BLASTED WORLD

The evolutions of cavalry and still more of aeroplanes are elementary compared to this. Close-packed as they are, a thousand of them will wheel in order without an accident and alight each on his own patch of ground with the easy grace of acrobats. It is only when they have found their feet that the disorder begins. Whether it is worms or insects or verdure they seek among the grazing cows, there is evidently little enough to go round, and starling fights starling with peck and protest all over the field. It is a scene of civil war, save that the birds do not form themselves into sides but each wrestles with its neighbour at random. But, after all, they are very hungry. They cluster ravenously on the green patches, even on the sides of the old stone walls. They have evidently not had the economic question settled for them as the cows have.

Luckily, other birds are either less desperate or more pacific by nature. The stone-chat as he flits from bramble to bramble in his black cap, white collar, and red bib is a bird of charming behaviour as well as of charming colour. There is nothing in him at discord with these rainbow days. For stormy as they are, the days are rain-

bow days to an astonishing extent. Seldom
have I seen such a violence of rainbows. The
colours almost startle one, like a courting ape's.
Every passing shower builds an arch of the
seven colours like a palace on the sea. Then
it draws near till the foot of the rainbow stands
a few yards below over the breaking waves.
Sea-birds sail through it, and, if a pot of gold
is really to be found at the end of it, I must
often lately have been within touching distance
of a fortune. . . . At night, Jupiter—it is
Jupiter, is it not? that hangs in the V of
Aldebaran about eight or nine in the evening
just now—stills the world to wonder as the
rainbow does by day. He is so splendid
a fire as to seem almost solitary, even when
the moon is shining. A few evenings ago, he
shed a path of light over the sea as the moon
does, and seemed to light up the sands
on the far side of the bay. . . . It is undoubtedly a blasted world, but what a beautiful blasted world! It is a pity that we and the
starlings are so belly-driven that we cannot
settle down to enjoy it. Peck, peck. My
worm, I think. Peck, peck, peck.

THE END